grief...

how long will you linger here?

...my life, my story.

by Linda Querry

Grief...how long will you linger here? My life...my story.
© Copyright 2023 Linda Querry

ISBN: 979-8-9873843-1-2 Paperback

Printed in the United States of America

This Book

The book you are about to read is about how I've reached the place I am today, five and a half years after I lost the love of my life. I share about our life from the beginning to the end as a couple, to the place I am today. I've also shared some flashbacks to when our three sons entered our lives.

I never planned to write this book. I began to journal every Thursday – the day of the week Chuck passed - week after week, and it became my therapy time. I would weep as I journaled, remembering the beautiful memories we had shared throughout our marriage. At some point during the end of that first year, I realized I couldn't stop journalling because these entries would help me remember, as long as I was on this earth, these very special times. Weeks turned into months, months turned into years, and with the encouragement from my family and so many of my friends, this book began.

Nobody can tell you what your grief feels like. Nobody can tell you how to move forward. All I can wish and pray for is that as you read this book, it helps you through the journey of grief you are on, which none of us made a reservation for.

CONTENTS

Chapter 1 *a magical beginning. . .* 1

Chapter 2 *is this blank wall my future?* 6

Chapter 3 *going home - alone* 12

Chapter 4 *the journey of real heartPAIN* that no one prepares you for... 18

Chapter 5 *I did not make a reservation for this trip* 22

Chapter 6 *widow? – me?* 27

Chapter 7 *. . .from this day . . .* 34

Chapter 8 *dropped in a jungle* 37

Chapter 9 *...and then there were three...* 46

Chapter 10 *tears, tears, & more tears* 50

Chapter 11 *did I just throat-punch you?* 53

Chapter 12 *footsteps into unknown paths* 58

Chapter 13 *and then there were four...* "Trusting God in the Storm...with small miracles along the way." 64

Chapter 14 *broken-heart syndrome* 73

Chapter 15 *and then there were five...* when God goes before you . . . 83

Chapter 16 *the many costumes of fear* 94

Chapter 17 *from grief to grace* 107

Chapter 18 *learn to dance with a limp* 119

Chapter 19 *tearing and mending* 124

Chapter 20 *dreams and/or visions* 127

Chapter 21 *"Pop" the hero in our family* **133**

Chapter 22 *life's a dance you learn as you go!* **150**

Chapter 23 *from the end...to the beginning* **156**

Scholarship Fund **161**

About the Author **162**

I Dedicate this book to...

First, to my loving husband, Charles (Chuck) Clifton Querry, who was my hero from the very beginning when we met and throughout the fifty-five years, "the wind beneath my wings." He loved me through the ups and downs and never ever failed to say, "I love you" every day. He made me believe I could fly above anything. Today he is flying with the angels.

Secondly, to our three sons, Kevin, Randy, and Rodney. They've always been great sons we've been proud of. They have each faced challenging times and been knocked down, but they were never knocked out. They always got back up and moved forward, accomplishing great things in their individual lives. During these past five-plus years, they have been strong for me even through their grief of losing their Pop. When I felt like I wanted to give up, just like their Pop would always do, they encouraged me, telling me more times than I can count, "Mom, you are strong; you can do this!"

Thirdly, to my daughters-in-law, Deena, Andi, and Nancy. Thank you all for opening up your homes when we needed a place to stay. Thank you for always being there for me through my tears these past five-plus years. Thank you for just sitting there at times and listening to me pour out my broken heart and never once making me feel I needed to get over it. Thank you for just being you – beautiful inside and out.

Fourthly, to our grandchildren: Nicolas, Daniel, Justin, Megan, Aubrey, Michael, Emily, and Hannah. You have brushed tears from my eyes. You have wrapped your arms around me, telling me I will make it. You have made me laugh until I cried. You have grown up to become beautiful inside and out, loving people and deeply loved by me, and never forget how much your Popa loved you.

And lastly, to our great-grandchildren: Austin Wade, Penelope Blake, Hazel Grace, Dakota Danielle, Ty Charles, Elijah Ray, and Ezekiel Dean. Oh, how your great Popa would have loved you. He would have bounced you on his knee, let you ride on his foot playing horsey until his leg wore out, and he would have sung silly songs and made-up songs with you every time he was with you. As I watch you grow up so fast, I often think of how much fun you would have had with your great Popa. But today, I will do my best to do double-time with hugs, kisses, and tons of love for the both of us.

Chapter 1

a magical beginning. . .

Christmas Eve, 1962

The rain was now dropping huge drops on the windshield of his pretty blue '57 Mercury, seemingly sounding louder than normal. But the thump. . .thump. . .thump of the rain helped occupy my mind and detour it from the sadness that had engulfed my heart. It was Christmas Eve, 1962. We pulled up in downtown Eugene, Oregon and parked beside a telephone booth. He was about to telephone his sister that he was on his way to Spokane, Washington to spend Christmas with her. As we hurried in the rain and crossed the sidewalk to the telephone booth, I shivered from the cold that now seemed worse than the rain. Pulling me up close, he wrapped his arm around me, in that tiny little phone booth, as he deposited one quarter after another into the phone slot and dialed the number. I could hear the phone ringing -one ring, two, three...maybe she wasn't home...then she answered. My mind wandered as they exchanged their small talk about the family. I fought the tears that were now swelling up inside me, knowing he would soon be leaving for the weekend. My mind quickly flashed to that Sunday afternoon two months ago at our first meeting.

It was October of 1962, my Senior year of High school, two weeks after my seventeenth birthday. I spent the afternoon that day with my girlfriend, Faye, my pastor's daughter. I loved going to her home on Sundays. It was a great break from the farm life and chores I'd normally have to do, yes, even on Sundays. Mucking stalls for the horses, cleaning rabbit cages, and sweeping the barn were no comparison to the afternoons between church services I'd get to spend with Faye and her family. We'd laugh and talk and laugh some more as we'd tell stories of how we thought our lives would be, and I wasn't going to live on a farm. I was going to New York and be a movie star, no maybe a flight attendant, oh no, definitely a dental assistant. Our chats were endless and I cherished the time we got to spend together.

This particular Sunday afternoon we were going to visit a co-worker of Faye's who'd been out sick for a week. The crunch of the fallen leaves under our feet was evidence that Fall was in the air. Red, orange, and yellow trees lined the sidewalk. I loved this season. The fresh, crisp cool air was refreshing and made me just want to skip a step or two. That feeling quickly changed as we knocked on the door of that little apartment. I felt nervous, and I hated meeting new people. Even though when Faye and I were together, our chatting was endless, I could never find words to say to someone I'd never met. In fact, it wasn't unusual for me to literally freeze, yet feel the heat rush through me just trying to speak out a hello. Within a nanosecond, I heard a voice say, "Come on in." Doors weren't locked during the days of 1962. As Faye opened the door, there he was. Sitting straight ahead of me in a baby blue sweater with his sleeves pushed up slightly between his wrist and elbows, watching a ball game on TV. I quickly noticed the Olympia beer sitting on the floor by his chair. That made me feel sick to my stomach. I had made myself a promise I'd never date or marry someone who drank. I'd lived around that with my dad, and I wasn't going there. Faye said hello and introduced me. In that moment our eyes locked, as he said hello with a smile on his face that melted my heart. Something magically happened, and for a moment, I forgot I was standing beside "my date." Faye, had set me up with him several weeks before on a blind date...it was definitely NOT magical and definitely not a match! As we walked over to the bedroom to pray for his sister, I wanted to just stay there, that one place at the door, looking at him. Why didn't Faye set me up on a blind date with him? Why did he have to drink? Why are my feet feeling like cement as Faye grabs my hand with a chuckle and pulls me with her. We prayed with his sister, and as we started to leave Faye invited him – yeah, that good looking guy – to come with us to church that night. I thought to myself, but he's a drunk, he's not going to go to church. But he did.

"Deposit another twenty-five cents to continue your call," I heard the shrill voice of the Operator say, as my mind snapped back to where I was that night. Fumbling in his pocket to find another quarter, I heard him say, "I know you're disappointed, sis, but I want to spend Christmas with Linda this year.

We had started dating just two weeks after that "love at first sight" meeting at his sister's apartment in October. He'd just gotten out of the Navy and was living with his sister. We were fifteen miles apart from his home to mine, and those miles meant a "long distance" telephone call to each other. We talked every other day for a few minutes each time. Weekends were great. Horseback riding, drives in the country, picnic lunches by a riverbank, and sharing ONE black raspberry milkshake with TWO straws was always the best way to end our weekends together. Now here we were ten weeks later, and he wanted to spend time with ME! He squeezed me tightly as he spoke those words to his sister. For the first time in the past twenty-four hours, I felt like my heart was about to explode with happiness instead of sorrow. He was spending Christmas with me!

They said their goodbyes, and with the rain still pouring down, we ran, hand in hand, back to his car. I slid into the driver's side of the car and stopped in the middle of that long seat with a smile across my face. Brushing the water from our coats, we began laughing. We were cold and wet, but none of that mattered now. He was spending Christmas with ME!

The laughter turned into numerous kisses. He kissed my lips, then my face, kissing all the water spots off. Then holding my face in his hands, he kissed my forehead and said, "Okay, stop for just a minute...". He reached over past me to the glovebox and took out a small white box. I thought my Christmas present? No, sweetheart, you'd just given me the BEST Christmas gift ever. I could see the glimmer in his eyes from the streetlights that shown above the car. "What are you doing Chuck Querry" I asked softly and suspiciously. He put his finger over my lips as he whispered, "ssshhh," and then proceeded to open that white box. Inside that small white box was a very little black box. I couldn't quit smiling; within a split second my mind wandered, traveling in every direction anyone could imagine. "Going steady?" "Promise Ring?" . . . then there in the moonlight – uh, I mean streetlights - sitting in his '57 Mercury, he opened that little black box. The sparkle of the ring told me immediately this was bigger than I thought. He looked into my eyes, and with a twinkle in his eyes that I came to see so many times, he said, "No flowering speeches. Linda, I love you and I want to spend the rest of my life with you, will you marry me?" My heart was beating so fast, my eyes now clouded by tears, there I was again, speechless. I'm not sure how long I just stared at that ring in his hand, until I jarred back to reality when I heard him say, "Well?" I didn't just speak softly this time, I screamed "YES! A thousand times YES! Yes! Yes! YES!" Tears were streaming down both our faces as we hugged each other tightly. He reached for his white handkerchief (something he always, always carried in his pocket till the very end) and gently wiping the tears from my eyes and then his, we sealed it with a kiss, and another and another... That cold rainy night was just "magical!" and only the beginning of fifty-five years of magical moments in our lives.

Chapter 2

is this blank wall my future?

June 22nd, 2017 – Sea Cliff Nursing Facility – 5:05 AM

I stood there just outside his room – numb – my back pressed against the wall - staring across the hallway at a blank wall . . . frozen in time, as if the clocks should stop ticking, the sun should stop shinning, the earth should stop spinning. The only thing I felt was the wet, very wet one after another, tears slowly and silently trickling down my trembling cheeks, dripping off my chin, now wetting my blouse. Our grandson, Daniel, also standing there staring at that blank wall, put his arm around me. That felt good; at least for a moment, I wasn't alone. I felt stiff, like I was frozen in time, yet even more sorrowful that he had lost his Papa. That made me feel sick at my stomach. My whole family was involved in this losing process that seemed impossible to process.

Just a few minutes before my phone had rung – louder than it's ever rang before. It shook me awake. I saw the caller ID – Sea Cliff Nursing Facility – where I'd left my husband sometime after midnight, it was 4:45 AM. I fumbled, trying to answer. I don't know if I said hello, the only thing I remember was hearing a nurse say, "you need to get here as quickly as you can; Charles is slipping away." Slipping away? NO! I felt a shockwave hit me like a thunderbolt hitting in a thunderstorm. I jumped to my feet, searching for my clothes...oh yeah, they were still on me. I hadn't undressed when I laid down a few hours ago.

I didn't even want to leave the facility that night, but my oldest son insisted I needed to go home and rest. He'd driven me to my middle son's home, where I had been staying since Chuck had been hospitalized seventeen days earlier. I heard my son shout from his bedroom, "Mom, is it Pop?" I somehow muttered the words, "Yes - hurry!" It felt like he took forever as I paced in the hallway of his home. Then in a moment, we were on our way. The 15-minute drive seemed much longer that morning. The radio was playing some country western song. My son told me later it was "My Old Man" by Zac Brown, and although he never had and never would refer to his "Pop" as "my old man," he had fought tears hearing it that morning because now he was living that song. I never heard a word of the song. My mind seemed fogged as if a heavy fog had settled in over my brain, my throat felt clogged, and I couldn't speak. My son was a Police Officer, and he could drive fast, but it wasn't fast enough for me that morning. All I remember is thinking, "Hurry, Randy, hurry..." but, I don't know if those words ever came out of my mouth. I vaguely remember leaving the car when we arrived...did I walk? Run? Stumble?

Then there I was, standing in front of Room 104...I remember that room number because that was our apartment number in "our" home. It seemed to be flashing that morning as if saying, "Sweetheart, take me home. . ." But that morning - my sweetheart, my Babe, my kids' Pop, my grandkids' Popa, my church's pastor, my friend's friend, my best friend, my lover, my soul-mate, my hero - he had gone "home" – to his forever home. I stood by his bedside, but his eyes weren't opening now. I kissed his lips; he didn't kiss me back. I stood there, unable to move, looking at his lifeless body. I touched his face, then his arm, slowly moving my hands down his body as the warmth left... his leg, his feet, as his life was ebbing away. Now he was gone, flying with wings with the angels. His warm embrace around me was over. His warm, gentle kisses were gone. Around midnight just as he was drifting off to sleep, he whispered his last words to me, "Baby, don't ever forget how much I love you." That memory now edged into my head, seemed like it was shouting those words, but then drifting away soft and softer and then gone. He was gone. His body – that tent where he'd lived seventy-nine years – was slowly becoming cold. There'd be no one reaching out to hold my hand as we walked into a shopping place or just sitting in a car ride going anywhere, or nowhere. There'd be no one now to stand by my bathroom door asking, "Are you beautiful yet?" with that smirky look on his face. There'd be no one I could share my deepest thoughts, or hurts, or just ask for his advice – he was gone! Who's going to have the coffee ready when I wake up? Who's going to text me when I'm out telling me to bring him his favorite food? Who's going to call me early Sunday mornings to wake me up and say one of those "roses are red, violets are blue" made-up poems he'd do? Who?

Standing there staring at that blank wall, there were no sounds coming from my trembling lips, yet inside me, I could hear my heart screaming, "Nooooooooo!!" This happens to someone else. NOT ME! Not us! Not my family! But it did! I tried to imagine Jesus with His arms reaching out, ready to wrap him up and hold him tightly as He welcomed him back to his eternal home. I wondered what heaven must be like . . . are they dressed casually or in a suit and tie like my sweet, handsome husband wore almost every day. Was there a golf course? Oh, how he loved a good game of golf. Are they singing? He had the most magnificent voice. Oh yes, there must be singing, and maybe just now he was bowing at the feet of Jesus singing with the angels, "How great Thou art, how GREAT THOU Aarrrrrtttttt...", holding that last note as long as he could.

I didn't see into heaven that Friday afternoon when he saw it twelve days earlier. A look came on his face that day, and I knew he was looking at something he'd never seen before. I asked him, "Babe, what are you looking at?" With his voice soft and sure, he said, "There ain't nothing bad up here. It's joy unspeakable. It's so beautiful here." Those following twelve days every time I'd ask "how are you, Babe?" His answered was always, "It's so beautiful here, sweet-heart." As those thoughts and memories flashed through my mind that morning, maybe, for a moment, it made the pain lessen... at least for a while. No truer words were ever pinned than these:

> **"I now exist somewhere between the pain of your death and the joy of your life."** [1]

That's where I was.

---

1 Quote attribution unknown

I don't know how long I stood there staring at that blank wall. In my head I felt it was screaming at me, "That is your future now. That's your 'new normal'." I didn't ask for a "new" normal. I was perfectly satisfied, fulfilled completely with my regular normal. We were supposed to grow old/er together. We talked so many times about how we'd retire and sit on a front porch in our rocking chairs, rocking away together. If one quit rocking, the other would rock them until they were able to rock again. But we'd be together forever. Now who's gonna rock my rocking chair? Now, here I am, stunned. Shocked! In a Fog! Empty! Scared! Most of all ALONE, yet with so many family members around me, I was still ALONE!

I don't know how I walked out of that facility that day. I'm pretty sure it could be best compared to that poem and picture of "Footprints in the Sand" by Mary Stevenson. There was only one set of footprints that morning leaving Sea Cliff Nursing Facility. I wasn't the one doing the walking; Jesus was carrying me out.

My Old Man - By Zac Brown
He was a giant, and I was a kid
I was always trying, to do everything he did.
I can still remember every lesson he taught me
Growing up learning how to be, like my old man.

He was a lion, we were our father's pride
But I was defiant, when he made me walk the line.
He knew how to lift me up, and when to let me fall
Looking back, he always had a plan, my old man.

My old man, feel the callous on his hands
And dusty overalls, my old man
Now I finally understand, I have a lot to learn
From my old man

Now I'm a giant, got a son of my own
He's always trying to go everywhere I go.
Do the best I can to raise him the right way
Hoping that he someday wants to be
Like his old man.

My old man, I know we'll meet again
As he's looking down, my old man
I hope he's proud of who I am
I'm trying to fill the boot of my old man.[2]

---

2 The song My Old Man was written by Zac Brown, Niko Moon and Ben Simonetti and
was first released by Zac Brown Band in 2017

Chapter 3

going home - alone

July 5th, 2017 – 13 days later

I don't remember that four-hour trip driving home – even though I was behind the wheel, I'm convinced God was the one driving. As I pulled in under the carport, once again, my entire body was frozen. Not even sure how long I sat there, but somehow, I eventually managed to get out of the car. As I turned, there was his car. Standing there looking at it, unable to move, as if I thought it should respond somehow. The car I'd look out the window every day and watch for him to turn in so I could set lunch or dinner on the table. The car that would take him to work and bring him home safely to me day after day, would now sit in a spot unmovable for a time. My knees felt like I was going to collapse. I struggled to just get to the front door of "our" apartment, "our" home. My hands were trembling as I tried to put the key in the door. Click, it finally connected, and the door was opened. I slowly dropped the bags I was carrying, which I'd forgotten were even in my hands, as I struggled to get to "his" chair. The pillows that had supported his back and hip were still in the chair. I hugged them tight to my chest and then pulled

them even tighter to my face to stifle the loud uncontrollable sobs that now poured out of my body. I don't remember
how long I cried – minutes – hours – days – yes, all of those.
Somehow, in the next few days, I finally managed to move
myself out of his chair and unload my car. Tears were still
dripping from my face as I carried in all his clothes, clothes
that he was supposed to come home in, clothes that he'll
never wear again. His medicine – pills that were supposed
to make him better – they failed! I even felt like I had failed.
If only I had forced him to go to the doctor when his hip
started hurting two years before. If only our doctors would
have done something sooner. If only.... if only...

The next few days are just a blurry vision. I cried. I wept.
And then I'd cry some more. Somewhere in the midst of
this Niagara Falls of tears, I managed to go through photo
albums to find pictures that would capture who he was for
his Celebration of Life service. Pictures that would show
that kind, loving, fun, funny Pop to our boys, Popa to our
grandkids, servant of God, that gentle giant, that man with a
"shepherd's" heart to find the lost and bring them home, that
incredible loving husband. How do you show, on a video, 55
years of the wonderful man you were, Babe? My sweetheart,
my hero, my strength in times of trouble, my confidant with
whom I could share my secrets, my counselor who could talk
me through difficult times, my best friend, my Pastor. The
man so many called Pop-not only our three sons but those
he'd become "Pop" to, Popa, Pastor, Dad, friend, mentor,
teacher, leader. There aren't enough photos to capture the
incredible life you lived, Babe, before anyone who knew
you...the legacy you left to anyone who crossed your path.

Somehow in those next few days, I managed to collect a collection of memories...I smiled as I looked at our wedding pictures. I smiled today when I heard our favorite song on the radio.... *"I'm gonna love you forever, forever and ever amen. As long as old men sit and talk about the weather; as long as old women sit and talk about old men.... I'm gonna love you forever and ever, forever and ever, amen."* [3]

Today, I smiled, remembering how I totally surprised you (and believe me, surprising Chuck was nearly impossible) as I "kidnapped" you in the car and drove you to the docks, where we went on our Catalina anniversary getaway. I remembered how we danced in our room that night to "our song." Then the many times we danced in our living room without even a song playing flooded my mind now. There were so many times, so, so many that I can't count, when we'd both be sitting in the living room, no one saying a word, and he'd jump to his feet, grab my hands and pull me to my feet and we'd just dance. I'd say, "Babe, there's no music," and he'd say, "There is if you'll quit talking and listen closely." I smiled today. But it's very possible tomorrow, I'll cry.

The nights were sleepless. The days were sorrowful. And in the midst of all of this fogginess, the church where we were pastoring voted 100% for me to continue as their Pastor. No! Stop! Not me! I'm a Pastor's wife – he was the Pastor. I can't fill his shoes. No! I can't do it – and that's my final answer! "There I said that!" (My very special friend, Brandy, taught me that phrase.) But it wasn't final. My State Overseer somehow convinced me that a hurting church congregation needed me – me? - to help them through the

---

3 Forever and Ever, Amen, written by Paul Overspreet and Don Schlitz, recorded by Randy Travis 1987

loss of "their" Pastor. I loved these people more than words. So, I gave him my "final" answer again, "I'll do it for 90 days, and then I'm done." I accepted the role of Lead Pastor on July 8th, 2017...my State Overseer, Charles Fischer, agreed but appointed me for four years, with the agreement that if, at the 90-day mark I wanted to leave, I could.

As alone as I felt, looking back, this was without a doubt the wisest decision I made after losing the love of my life. My mind was clouded. My heart still hurt. My eyes were swollen. Yet, during those times as a Pastor, I can truly say there were a lot of "Footprints in the Sand" moments.

So many Sundays, I cried all the way driving to church. Sitting in my car taking, deep breaths, and praying, "God, if you don't help me, this will be the end today." I'd get out of the car, and a calm peacefulness would come over me like I'd never felt before. I'd play the piano, sing and lead worship, and deliver my sermon, never feeling my feet on the floor. After everything was done, I'd get back in my car and feel like a ton of bricks had just landed on my chest, and would cry all the way home. Every Sunday for months, this was me. Me being carried in the arms of Jesus. Then gradually, as I began to learn to walk again, I was like that toddler – slowly getting my balance, even walking on tiptoes at times – knowing within my heart that God was standing right there beside me, supporting me until I could walk again and ready to catch me if I fell. In time, I was able to even run a short distance...but I could never have done it myself. If I was still breathing, if I was still moving, then there must be more of "my" story to tell. I just needed to finish the book God wrote about me before I was conceived. No one will ever make me believe that it wasn't God there, steadying me, giving me His wisdom in difficult decisions, giving me the strength every day to just get out of bed.

The Psalmist wrote, *"Your eyes saw my unformed substance; and in Your book all the days [of my life] were written before ever they took shape, when as yet there was none of them."* (Psalm 139:16 AMPC)

There is no preparation kit for the death of a loved one. There's nothing you can do to emotionally prepare yourself for its arrival. When the doctor told us he had "six months," the shock of denial of those words kicked in full speed in my brain. I refused to accept it. My husband's words were, "It'll be okay, sweetheart; we'll beat this!" The doctors told us we needed to call in Hospice. HOSPICE? Why? We'll beat this! Just like I refused to believe in his death, without a handbook, or a class on how to handle it, when it hit, it felt like a blow to my gut, and the wind had just been knocked out of me. NOBODY prepared me for it! I don't care how many doctors looked me in the eye and gave me his death sentence, NOBODY prepared me for what I was about to face.

Grief doesn't come tapping softly on your door. It brings a sledgehammer with a loud jolt saying, "I'm here!" There isn't a timeframe, like you get so many strikes and you're out, or a time clock runs out and the game of grief is over. Oh, yeah, there's always someone who makes it their duty to tell you, "You'll get over this," or "This is your 'new' normal," or "They're in a better place!" Death is PERSONAL! Your journey is your journey. Friends don't know what to do with our pain. Loved ones struggle, trying to comfort us with words they can't even find. And just about the time you think you're doing better, another monstrous wave sweeps you off your feet and forces you to the floor in tears or to your bed, smothering your sobs in a pillow so no one can hear you.

Yet, in all of this, grief is a necessary part of our healing. As difficult as it is, you can't shut it up inside you, and you can't run from it and be healed in it. You and your spouse were a completed puzzle, fitly completed and joined together. When we lose one, the puzzle is dumped upside down, and the pieces are thrown everywhere. We will gradually put the pieces of our puzzle back together, but there will always be that one missing piece. That spot where that piece is missing will remind us that was the place your missing loved one filled.

In time – so give yourself time – all the time you need – we all find a way to pick up the pieces and move forward. To do this, we have this promise from Isaiah 41:10 (NIV):

"So do not fear, for I am with you; do not be dismayed, for I am your God. I will strengthen you and help you..."

Chapter 4

the journey of real heartPAIN
that no one prepares you for...

3 weeks after your journey to heaven, Babe – July 15, 2017

Grief: anguish, suffering, pain, agony, torment, heartbreak, misery, grief-stricken, sorrow, woe, sadness, unhappiness, desolation, despair . . .the list in the dictionary goes on and on. But until you experience it, no one can describe your individual grief. I seem to have them all:

Pain/Heartache: As I sat in a bleacher tonight watching my son's softball team play, I couldn't take my eyes off "the chair" where my husband sat at every game – now draped with a Querry Warrior's jersey – but he's not there.

Anguish/Sorrow/Sadness: As I cradled my little 10-year-old granddaughter, Hannah, in my arms as she wept because she was missing her Popa – no "we" wept...knowing this time "I" couldn't fix it. When she opened her photo album to show me a "visitor sticker" she'd gotten at the hospital when she went to visit her Popa – now unable to detect what it was because it'd gone through the wash and stuck to her pajamas – but she knew what it was, and was keeping it safely tucked in the back of her photo album. Twelve weeks later, September 13, 2017, Hannah wrote this poem about her Popa.

"Love"
by Hannah Querry at 10 years old

It's not goodbye forever,
It's just 'til we meet again
It's not you used to love me
It's you'll love me 'til the end.

Sometimes I wonder why you had to go
But then I realized what I didn't know
You're in a better place now
Where you can never be harmed again.
With all my heart, I'll love you
And I'll love to the end.

And to all my family members
That have sadly passed away
I have loved you forever
And I love you to this day!

Desolation/Despair/Unhappiness: As I sat in a restaurant tonight with a group of softball players and their families, hearing their laughter - that seemed like it was buildings away – feeling alone, empty, knowing Babe in times past "we" – the you-me "we" - sat there entering into that laughter.

Heartbreak/Sorrow/Grief-stricken: The pain inside me never goes away. The heaviness in my heart doesn't lift. People tell me it will get better...will it? Will it always hurt? Will my legs always feel like they're made of cement – or Jell-O? Will my eyes always flood with tears when I mention your name? The silence is deafening! My prayers are speechless! In a room filled with people, I'm ALONE. My tears could fill an ocean! There are questions – but no answers!

Yet, in ALL of this – with everything within me – in my silent shout for help screaming from my insides, I'm reminded of the 23rd Psalm once again. God, as my Shepherd, leading and guiding me (a helpless sheep - stumbling along) to green pastures and still waters...prepares me a table...pours oil on my head/wounds...

WAIT! - WHAT?

God, are you telling me You've got THIS? "This" (me) is a MESS! But You, Lord, have "this" by the hand – leading "this" where the rumbling rolling water rapids of my heart will settle down and be STILL – that Your healing oil will somehow mend this open wounded broken heart??? I'm a cracked vase, God. I'm a broken vessel! I only have half a heart now because my other half went with Chuck to heaven. How can You mend half of a heart? I'm that mess!

Yet, tonight God, as I've pulled myself up off the floor, leaving a puddle of tears and grasping to pick up a box of wet-soaked Kleenex where I've been, I TRUST You, Lord. Somewhere in my mind of confusion, my brain pushes through all that and reminds me once again of Your words in the Bible:

"Your eyes saw me when I was formless; all my days were written in your book and planned before a single one of them began." (Psalm 139:16 CSB).

Does that mean You, Lord, KNOW I can survive "this?" Then for a moment, I could hear my husband's words that he'd tell our boys and me over and over in a tough time, "Keep Your Chin Up!" Then he'd tell us when your chin is up, you're looking towards the One who will help you through this. Tonight, those words are echoing in my ears. My chin is up, God, even if I'm having to prop it up. I trust Your leading because You know what my next chapter looks like.

Chapter 5

I did not make a
reservation for this trip

July 23, 2017 - following your Celebration of Life service

I t felt like a vice-grip had just been placed on my heart. I couldn't breathe, nor want to. I've never in my wildest dreams or imagination thought this kind of pain, hopelessness, or loneliness was possible. I've lost so many others in my life, but nothing even comes close to the pain I feel now. I keep shaking my head, thinking this is a nightmare. This isn't real. I'll hear your car drive in. You'll walk in the door again. I'll wake up. Then I realize I am awake! This. Is. Real! I won't hear the click of your shoes coming up the sidewalk. You won't walk in the door again. I won't smell the aroma of your cologne as you pass by me.

I sit in "our" home and look around, and all I can see is "STUFF!" None of it means anything to me now. I decorated it all for "us," but the "us" was gone. Now I want everything gone – yet I can't part with anything.

I can't stay focused. My mind keeps wandering into the heavenlies. What are you doing up there, Babe? Have you seen your family yet? Did you see my Mom and Dad? What's it like seeing Jesus face to face? Can you see me when I'm crying? Can you see my broken heart? You always knew when something was bothering me. Is this where you see me crying, and you cry too? Is this where Jesus wipes all the tears away from your eyes? I feel numb. Will I ever laugh again? Will I ever find happiness without you here? Who do I go do things with? Who's going to sit across the table with me in a restaurant for a special dinner? Who's going to carry the groceries from the car. Who's going to wake me up every morning with kisses? It was always you. I'm so messed up. How did I ever think I could help a church full of hurting people when I'm hurting? Am I losing my mind? Nobody prepared me for this. I tried to start your car today, but the battery is dead. Did it die because you died? How do I do this? How can I go on?

Celine Deon sings a song written by Diane Warren:

"Because you loved me."

"For all those times you stood by me. For all the truth that you made me see. For all the joy you brought to my life. For all the wrong that you made right. For every dream you made come true. For all the love I found in you. I'll be forever thankful baby, you're the one who held me up. Never let me fall. You're the one who saw me through it all.

"You were my strength when I was weak. You were my voice when I couldn't speak. You were my eyes when I couldn't see. You saw the best there was in me. Lifted me up when I couldn't reach. You gave me faith 'cause you believed. I'm everything I am because you loved me.

"You gave me wings and made me fly. You touched my hand I could touch the sky. I lost my faith; you gave it back to me. You said no star was out of reach. You stood by me and I stood tall. I had your love I had it all. I'm grateful for each day you gave me. Maybe I don't know that much, but I know this much is true, I was blessed because I was loved by you. **"** 4

Sweetheart, that's how I do it...I do it because you loved me. Because even when there are no words, when my tears are released in waves, I can't control, when this pain in my chest causes me to struggle till the next breath... I know I can do it because you took this seventeen-year-old young girl, who was so shy I could barely look anyone in the eyes, and you made me the person I am today. You were my voice when my words weren't spoken. You took my insecurities and convinced me I could do anything because I had God on my side. You saw me better than I ever saw myself – until I met you, dreams that were only in my imagination, you brought them to life. So even knowing all this, I still ask when does it stop hurting? When do I stop crying? When will my life be "normal" again?

I found this writing, "Old Man's View of Grief" ...and it has given me more clarity than anyone else has been able to.

"Old Man's View of Grief"
" As for grief, you'll find it comes in waves. When the ship is first wrecked, you're drowning, with wreckage all around you. Everything floating around you reminds you of the beauty and the magnificence of the ship that was, and is no more. And all you can do is float. You find some piece of the wreckage and you hang on for a while. Maybe it's some physical thing. Maybe it's a happy memory or a photograph. Maybe

---

4   "Because You Loved Me" was written by Diane Warren and produced by David Foster. Performed by Canadian singer Celine Dion on her fourth English-language studio album, *Falling into You* (1996)

it's a person who is also floating. For a while, all you can do is float. Stay alive.

"In the beginning, the waves are 100 feet tall and crash over you without mercy. They come 10 seconds apart and don't even give you time to catch your breath. All you can do is hang on and float. After a while, maybe weeks, maybe months, you'll find the waves are still 100 feet tall, but they come further apart. When they come, they still crash all over you and wipe you out. But in between, you can breathe, you can function.

"You never know what's going to trigger the grief. It might be a song, a picture, a street intersection, the smell of a cup of coffee. It can be just about anything...and the waves comes crashing. But in between waves, there is life.

"Somewhere down the line, and it's different for everybody, you find the waves are only 80 feet tall. Or 50 feet tall. And while they still come, they come further apart. You can see them coming. An anniversary, a birthday, or Christmas, or landing at O'Hare. You can see it coming for the most part, and prepare yourself. And when it washes over you, you know that somehow you will, again, come out on the other side. Soaking wet, sputtering, still hanging on to some tiny piece of the wreckage, but you'll come out.

"Take it from an old guy. The waves never stop coming, and somehow you don't really want them to. But you learn that you'll survive them. And other waves will come. And you'll survive them too. If you're lucky, you'll have lots of scars from lots of loves. And lots of shipwrecks. 🗝🗝 [5]

5 Popovic, Bobby. "He Was Grieving over the Death of His Best Friend, until an Old Man Told Him This. Mind Blown." Tickld, 28 Oct. 2021, www.tickld.com/heartwarming/1848120/old-man-explains-death-and-life-to-grieving-young-man/.

Here I am today, with more shipwrecks and one-hundred-feet waves than I can count. Pieces of the wreckage still show up quite often, giving me something I can hang on to until the waves level out again. Some days are just "crashes and hard hits" that bring me to a breakdown of tears. . . and just when I think I'll never recover, God is there. He reaches down, picks me up from the puddle of snot and tears, wipes my eyes, blows my nose, dusts me off, and, what seems beyond belief, gives me the strength to stand up on my feet again and carry on a little farther on this endless journey – that I didn't make a reservation to travel...and no one asks to take.

Chapter 6

widow? – me?

There I was, sitting in the lobby of the Social Security office, frozen at the question in front of me on a piece of paper. All I had to do was circle one word - married, single, widow? WIDOW – that word echoed at me as if everyone in the lobby had heard it and was looking at me. WIDOW . . . doesn't that mean your husband is dead? Now that word had gone from 12-font to 72-font on that sheet of paper! All I could see was the word "WIDOW" flashing at me like a neon sign. I felt like something had knocked my breath out of me. My face was flush with a burning heat. The walls of the room were closing in. I felt sick at my stomach. I think I'm going to throw up. I've got to get out of here. I felt myself wanting to run, but my legs felt like jelly. I gathered all the papers and searched in my purse for my keys. I felt faint. Where's my car? Where did I park? I was shaking out of control. Breathe, Linda, breathe, I kept telling myself. I hadn't had a panic attack in 45 years. Not since God had healed me after a nervous breakdown when I was in my mid-twenties. But a panic attack had attacked me all over one word that I couldn't seem to react to. WIDOW - is this what widowhood was like?

"Number 3 to Window 13... Number 3 to Window 13... last call for number 3, please go to Window 13" – WAIT! 3? That's me. That announcement that rang through that building shook me back once again to where I was. I stumbled as I stood to my feet, gathering up those papers. "Are you okay, miss?" the older man sitting next to me asked. I'm not even sure if I answered him. I tried to clear my mind as I franticly searched for Window 13... Miss? He just called me Miss? I'm not a "Miss"; I'm a "Mrs., right? No? Yes? I don't know - am I a WIDOW?"

Arriving at Window 13, the gentleman looked at me and asked, "Are you okay?" Shaking my head, no, trying to speak through the apple size lump that had now grown in my throat, I handed him the papers. Fighting with everything in me, I pointed to that horrific question - that for the first time, I was faced with answering, and said, "I don't know what to put there." He reached across the desk and took my hand. That was it, the tears just fell...one after another. He said, "It's okay, I've already pulled up your paperwork and completed that question while I was waiting for you." Through my wet face and my runny nose, I somehow managed to say to him, "Did you know my husband's number in sports was Number Thirteen?" "No," he replied, "but maybe your husband just directed you here to this window today to let you know you're not alone?"

I wiped my tears. He typed away. Within a few minutes, he told me everything was done and the amount my social security check would now be. Those numbers vanished from my mind as soon as he said them. He handed me copies of the paperwork and again took my hands in his hands and said, "Today, is a tough day for you, but God, just like today, will get you through all the tough days ahead." Then he said goodbye. I couldn't even remember his name, but I didn't want to say goodbye; I wanted to take him home with me. I wanted to keep him. He understood my tears. And for a few brief minutes, I didn't feel so all alone!

· · · · · · · · · · · · · ·

Alisha Bozarth, author and blogger, Hope Grows in the Wilderness, wrote this, **"Widowhood is More than . . ."**

" Widowhood is more than missing your spouse's presence. It is adjusting to an alternate life. It is growing around a permanent amputation.

"Widowhood is going to bed for the thousandth time and still, the loneliness doesn't feel normal. The empty bed a constant reminder. The night no longer brings intimacy and comfort, but the loudness of silence and the void of connection.

"Widowhood is walking around the same house you have lived in for years and it no longer feels like home. Because "home" incorporated a person. And they're not there. Homesickness fills your heart and the knowledge that it will never return haunts you.

"Widowhood is seeing all your dreams and plans you shared as a couple crumble around you. The painful process of searching for new dreams that include only you, amount to climbing Mount Everest. And every small victory of creating new dreams for yourself includes a new shade of grief that their death propelled you to this path.

"Widowhood is second guessing everything you thought you knew about yourself. Your life had molded together with another's and without them you have to relearn all your likes, hobbies, fears, goals. The renaissance of a new person makes you proud and heartbroken simultaneously. "Widowhood is being a stranger in your own life. The unnerving feeling of watching yourself from outside your body, going through the motions of what was your life, but being detached from all of it. You don't recognize yourself. Your previous life feels but a vapor long gone, like a mist of a dream you begin to wonder if it happened at all.

"Widowhood is the irony of knowing if that one person was here to be your support, you would have the strength to grieve that one person. The thought twists and confuses you. If only they were here to hold you and talk to you, you'd have the tenacity to tackle this unwanted life. To tackle the arduous task of moving on without them.

"Widowhood is missing the one person who could truly understand what is in your heart to share. The funny joke, the embarrassing incident, the fear compelling you or the frustration tempting you. To anyone else, you would have to explain, and that is too much effort, so you keep it to yourself. And the loneliness grows inside of you.

"Widowhood is struggling with identity. Who are you if not their spouse? What do you want to do if not the things you planned together? What brand do you want to buy if not the one you two shared for 20 years? What is your purpose if the job of investing in your marriage is taken away? Who is my closest companion when my other half isn't here?

"Widowhood is feeling restless because you lost your home, identity, partner, lover, friend, playmate, travel companion, co-parent, security, and life. And you are drifting with an unknown destination.

"Widowhood is living a constant state of missing the most intimate relationship. No hand to hold. No body next to you. No partner to share your burden.

"Widowhood is being alone in a crowd of people. Feeling sad even while you are happy. Feeling guilty while you live. It is looking back while looking forward. It is being hungry, but nothing sounding good. It is every special event turning bittersweet.

"Yes. It is much more than simply missing their presence. It is becoming a new person, whether you want to or not. It is fighting every emotion mankind can feel at the very same moment and trying to function in life at the same time.

"Widowhood is frailty. Widowhood is strength. Widowhood is darkness. Widowhood is rebirth.

"Widowhood . . . is life changing. 🔳🔳 6

Alisha Bozarth, if I didn't know better, I could easily believe you had just interviewed me and written down every word I had said.

EVERYTHING about my life has changed. I'm not the same person I was when I was with Chuck. On my darkest, toughest days, times, and trials, when I was out of control with my emotions, he could talk me into a calmness. I can't tell you the times I've been venting and ended up in tears. Those times when I felt like my world had just come crashing down at my feet. He'd get up from where he was sitting, (usually leaned back in his recliner) where seconds before he was just quietly chilling. Now he was listening intently to every word I was saying. He'd walk over to me, wrap me up in his arms, and let me cry a few more tears. Then he'd

6 Bozarth, Alisha. "Widowhood Is More Than…" Alisha Bozarth, Author and Blogger, 28 Feb. 2020, alishabozarth.com/2018/12/23/widowhood-is-more-than/.

take out his white handkerchief, wipe my eyes, and I'd cry even more. He'd wipe more tears. When he thought I was ready – or he was - he'd take his hand, lift my chin and say, "That's enough. Everything is going to be alright." If I didn't stop then, he'd start singing me one of his "made-up" silly songs – and then another verse – and then another – oh, how I wish I'd written down those songs, but he'd never stop until he had me laughing. Now here I am, and he is gone! Who's gonna wipe my eyes now? Who's gonna sing me silly songs now? Who's gonna hold me and calm me down and make me believe "everything is going to be alright?"

There are days when I'm convinced there is no more liquid in my body to make one more tear... and there is. As I write this today, I'm reminded that our tears never go unnoticed by God. Psalm 56:8 (NLT) declares this:

"You keep track of all my sorrows. You have collected all my tears in Your bottle. You have recorded each one in Your book."

I'm pretty sure God must have enlarged the room where He's collecting all my tears to make room for all the bottles.

Can you just imagine that? The God of this Universe, hearing millions of prayers at any given time, is aware of every tear that leaves your eyes. Jesus knows the hurt of losing someone. When His friend Lazarus died – even though He knew He would live again, the Gospel of John, chapter 11, verse 35 says, *"Jesus wept."* Isaiah 53:3 tells us that Jesus was *"a man of sorrows and acquainted with grief."*

As I travel this journey of grief, I know this one thing for sure: that in my deepest heart-breaking moments of nothing but tears, God has stopped by my room with a bottle in His hands to collect my tears and with His Book and pen to record them. Don't ever think, in your loneliest, tearful times, that you're alone. There. Right. Beside. You. Is God! Standing close enough to you to catch every teardrop that falls from your eyes and then record it in His book.

Chapter 7

...from this day ...

Friday evening, April 12th, 1963.
Four months after that night on Christmas Eve

"... I take you, Charles, to have and to hold from this day forward. . ."... my knees were shaking so hard I knew everyone could hear them, and my voice was quivering as I softly spoke these words. Is every ceremony this long? Those words flashed through my mind as I stood there looking into his brown eyes – the man of my dreams...am I dreaming? Am I going to wake up, and nothing of this moment happened? For a moment I felt like I was having an "out of the body" experience until I heard the minister say, "I now pronounce you husband and wife; you may kiss your bride." No, I wasn't dreaming. This was real! My knees stopped shaking as he wrapped me up in his arms. His lips touched mine, and with a kiss that made my heart melt, it was sealed. We were man and wife.

As we walked, very fast, down the church aisle of that little Open Bible Church that night, Chuck leaned over, squeezing me closer to him, and whispered in my ear, "Let's get out of here!" Looking up at him, I saw the biggest smile across his face. We chuckled – that's exactly what we wanted to do.

In all my recent girlfriend's weddings, it had become a "thing" for the bridal party to "kidnap" the bride and hide her away that first night, then return her to the church the next day. Chuck had told me several times that that was NOT going to happen to him. But we couldn't leave yet – we had our reception to show up at.

After the cutting of the cake, I slipped away to the bridal room and changed from my wedding dress into my "going-away" white suit – that was also a "thing" to do in the '60's. Walking back into the church where Chuck was waiting, he again took my hand and said, "NOW, let's get out of here!" We made a mad dash for the door, him holding me close to his side, our arms locked together tightly, dashing through the pelting of the rice being thrown at us by our screaming relatives and friends. I didn't even notice the soft sprinkling of rain that was falling, making his blue '57 Mercury sparkle in the streetlights. Quicky, we jumped into the car, locked the doors, and within seconds, we were off. The clanging of the tin cans tied to the back bumper of our beautifully decorated car and the non-stop honking of the cars following us was almost deafening. Nothing, and no one, was stopping Chuck that night. "Hang on, sweetheart," he said as we turned and dashed down a side street and then another and another. The sound of screeching tires around every corner was scary. Then as the honking horns slowly drifted out of earshot, we slowed down. Somewhere making those sharp turns, the clanging tin cans had broken loose from the bumper, and there we were – free! We laughed so hard...we were on our way to our "honeymoon."

Our "honeymoon" was different than they are today. Short – and close by. We drove for an hour to a little place in Cottage Grove, Oregon, and checked in to our hotel – well, err, "motel." This was just the beginning of "our" story. We didn't have a clue to the adventurous, exciting, unknowing, wonderful fifty-four years, two months, and ten days that lay ahead of us that night.

As I write this today, I'm reminded of the song sung by Andy Williams, **"The Impossible Dream."**

> **"** To dream the impossible dream, to fight the unbeatable foe. To bear with unbearable sorrow, to run where the brave dare to go.
> "To right the un-rightable wrong. To love pure and chaste from afar. To try when your arms are to weary, to reach the unreachable star.
> "This is my quest, to follow that star. No matter how hopeless, no matter how far. To fight for the right without question or pause, to be willing to march into hell for a heavenly cause. And I know if I'll only be true to this glorious quest, that my heart will lie peaceful and calm, when I'm laid to rest.
> "And the world will be better for this, that one man, strong and covered with scars, still strove with his last ounce of courage, to fight the unbearable foe. To reach the unreachable star. **"** [7]

This was Charles Querry. This was us! This was our impossible dream! And a dream that became more than a "dream"; it became "our life." As I reflect back on these years, not now, not ever, have I had any regrets. At the closing chapter of his book, the book God wrote about him, on June 22, 2017, I will forever be thankful I was the one he chose to live his impossible dream with, "...till death we do part."

---

7 The Impossible Dream; composed by Mitch Leigh, with lyrics written by Joe Darion, performed by Andy Williams, 1968

Chapter 8

dropped in a jungle

#twomonthsangelversary – August 22, 2017

The darkness surrounds me, blinding me and making it hard to see where I am going. I stumble along trying desperately to surpass the "stuff" that has me entrapped here. I search to remember the sounds I've been familiar with...waking up to the sound of coffee flowing through the coffee maker, the hair dryer blowing after his morning shower, hearing him whistling as he was doing something around the house, the sound of him praying in the living room as he knelt by his chair before starting every day and leaving the house, the click of his springy footsteps coming up the sidewalk to our door (I could spot him in a crowd anywhere, just looking for the man with a bounce in his steps). I clasped my hands over my ears, trying to stifle out the "new" sounds I now hear. The silence seems to scream at me. There's no coffee making in the morning, and the hair dryer lies silently on the bathroom shelf. The only praying I hear now is me crying out, "OH GOD WHY? WHY ME? WHY US?...coming from my lips. The Bible is closed. I can't see the words now because of my swollen tear-filled eyes.

Nothing seems real! I'm driving home after a day of running errands and appointments, and looking at my watch, it was five o'clock. "Oh no," I think, "I've got to get home and get dinner. Chuck will be home soon. . ." and for a millisecond, my mind had flashed back to what I was familiar with. Times when I reach for my phone to text him or check my phone to see if he's texted me. These swift moments are the mind trickery that continues to take my breath away. It's not fair; it's cruel that, at my very core, I still can't remember that he's gone. Someone called it "grief amnesia" – it's a real thing.

I try to stay busy, go somewhere, do something, anything because I know when I walk into "our" home, this stranger that I'm becoming quite familiar with will be there; "Grief." I've come to hate you, Mr. Grief. It's you reminding me he's not coming home! Not tonight, not ever! I turn on the TV because the silence is too loud to bear. I don't eat, I'm not hungry, and he's not here for me to cook his favorite foods. He won't be home soon; he's not going to walk in the door again. I crash again into a puddle of tears. How am I going to get out of this mess of a jungle I feel like I've been dropped into? I feel lost, trapped in a place I don't want to be, yet, have no clue on how to get out.

• • • • • • • • • • • • • •

I've learned some things that nobody told me:
  † That no matter how prepared you think you are for death, you can never be prepared for the grief that follows.
  ♥ I'll never forget Hospice and the doctor telling me I had to "release" my husband to go to his

eternal home. That night before he passed, I leaned over and whispered in his ear, because I couldn't stand to see him suffer any more pain, "Babe, if you want to go be with Jesus, I'll be "alright!" Ba-hum-bug! That was the biggest lie I'd ever told my husband – even though I "thought" I believed it when I said it. I was never and still am not "alright!" His words to me that night after I said that was, "Sweetheart, don't ever forget how much I love you." "Those" are the words that keep me going. Those last words of his that I cling to daily. Never in my wildest dreams or imaginations did I have any clue on that night of the journey I was about to travel.

† Death and grief make people uncomfortable. Be prepared to be isolated from some of your "close" friends and family.

† People will bring you food because they're trying to help – don't feel bad throwing it away.

† Regrets will always show up in your head – you'll always wish you had more time or used the time you had with each other better.

♥ Do you know how many times I've regretted "releasing him to go be with Jesus?" They're too many to count!

† Grief is messy and confusing. The fogginess in your brain is normal. You're not going crazy.

♥ Nobody! Nobody told me that! There were times, no days.... weeks... when I thought I was losing my mind...until someone told me who'd recently lost their husband, "Linda, you're not going crazy; I feel the same way." No, they weren't a counselor or a therapist; she was a woman grieving just like me, who made me feel like maybe I wasn't going cray-cray!

† However badly you think it's going to hurt, believe me it's a gazillion times worse than you imagine.

† Take note that you will never be the same person again.

♥ The hardest thing for me to grasp is that the "old" me is gone. She went with him to heaven. But somewhere inside me, as lost as I feel at times, there is a "new" me – and before you think it, I was perfectly happy with the "old" me! – but I have to accept she died too. Inside this body which still looks exactly like me on the outside, is a changed person begging to be discovered. She is probably unrecognizable to those who have known me in the past, and she's only emerging a little at a time. This world which she thinks should have stopped spinning, has to give her time to react to this new person she's not fully acquainted with yet. I miss that "old" me – the happy me – the me that felt secure because it was the "you and me" "we." That part of her still struggles to wish that part of her life back again. You can recognize it in her eyes in pictures, the sadness that still struggles to change.

† Time doesn't heal all wounds.

♥ Grief is real. Heartbreak is real heartPAIN! And it doesn't have a time limit. My life is now lived every day in a "one-day-at-a-time" scenario...a statement that a very close friend and "family of choice" told me often during those first few months/now years. (Bobby, you will never know how much your phone calls every week kept me going, and you telling me this every time.)

♥ At times I feel like I've passed this time, only to discover another puddle of tears and another one-hundred-foot wave that's knocked me to the floor again. Then, for a while, my feet move much slower for a few days until I can get up to speed again.

The foundation of "me" as I knew it, crumbled the day my lover, my best friend, my soul-mate got his wings. Now there's a "Caution, Entering Work Zone" sign flashing where I'm rebuilding in this jungle I've been dropped into. There are and have been days that have been hellish. There are days of just clearing a pathway. There are times that it's four blocks up – two blocks down. Six blocks up – three blocks down...slowly progressing. There are potholes, and at times it even feels like I've stepped in quicksand, sinking before anyone can get me out – or days that I don't even want to get out – but I do.

. . . .

There's a well-known trap used by hunters to catch a monkey.

They get a coconut and cut a hole inside the coconut – empty it out - they make the hole just big enough so the monkey's hand can fit in the hole – but the fist can't.

Inside the coconut they place fruit or nuts to lure the monkeys. Then they tie the coconut to the tree and wait.

What they've found is that the monkeys are greedy!

The monkey sticks its little hand inside the coconut to pull a handful of fruit out but can't get it out.

When the hunter approaches, they try even harder to pull their fists out with the fruit, but they can't. And they're captured.

All that monkey had to do was open its hand and turn loose of what was in its hand, and it would be free.

But his desire to hold on to what's in his hand blinds him to his freedom. His attachment to that object is so strong that he sacrifices his life for it.

. . . .

Silly monkeys – RIGHT?

Hummmm - - - - maybe not?

What is in your coconut?

What are you holding on to in your hand that you won't turn loose of?

What if you could just let it go – and you'd be free!

What are you refusing to give up?

What are you hanging on to for dear life and sacrificing your own life for?

I know what it feels like to try and "hold on" to what was, and I also know that it's extremely hard to try and move past it.

Grief is real! Grief is necessary! Grief, to some point, will always be a part of your life because of your loss.

But there's one Commander in charge of this rebuilding "me" project with a "blueprint" and "roadmap" I desperately try to follow. I can rest assured that if I follow and trust it

I will accomplish what I'm supposed to. That blueprint... that roadmap...is God's Word – the Bible. That Commander in charge is my Lord and Savior, Jesus Christ. That's who I cling to as I travel this bumpy road of rebuilding my life when I can't understand any of it. When everything seems all tangled up. When the darkness around me makes if feel like there is no way out. When I feel the pothole or sinkhole I've fallen into will engulf me. It's in those moments that I look closely at this roadmap and read in Psalms 46:1 and 10 [NIV]: (1) *God is our refuge and strength, a very present help in trouble... (10) "Be still, and know that I am God."*

It's His words that calm me down when I feel like I'm sitting in a chair screaming and kicking my feet because this journey isn't easy.

It's Him that helps me release my grip of what I'm holding on to in this "coconut" of life that keeps me from moving forward.

I can't do it! But He is my strength! I want to run and hide. He is my refuge, and into His arms, I can run. There, He encourages me, telling me,

"For I know the plans I have for you (Linda), *plans to prosper you and not harm you, plans to give you a hope, and a FUTURE!* (Jeremiah 29:11 NIV)

Then He tells me,

"For my thoughts (Linda) are not your thoughts, neither are your ways my ways...as the heavens are higher than the earth, so are My ways higher than your ways, and My thoughts [higher] than your thoughts. (Isaiah 55:8.9 NIV)

It's with those words I can take a deep breath and for a moment, *"be still and know He is God"* (Psalm46:10 NIV), and He's got me and my life, even in this dark jungle, under control.

I've been studying in a Bible Study group the book of Daniel. In chapter four, Nebuchadnezzar has had a dream and needs it to be interrupted. As he relates the dream to Daniel, he tells how he saw an enormous tall tree. The leaves were beautiful, and the fruit was good and plentiful. But then he sees a messenger from heaven, and he tells him to cut down the tree. In verse 15 he says, *"But let the stump and its roots, bound with iron and bronze remain in the ground in the grass of the field."* [8] Now if you read the whole message, you'll see where Daniel tells Nebuchadnezzar his fate. But the thing that stopped me in my tracks as I read this was that even though Nebuchadnezzar was about to lose everything, God saw beyond that devastation, and He loved him enough to preserve him. God chose to leave the stump of that "tree" (Nebuchadnezzar), and its roots, and He protected that part by surrounding it with iron and bronze, in the grass of that field. Read the whole story, and you'll see where Nebuchadnezzar was restored to be even greater than he was before.

I don't know about your loss, but when I lost Chuck, I felt like I'd just lost everything! I felt like I was cut down to a stump! But when I read this passage, my heart was impacted by this short little statement. I felt like God reminded me that the "stump" of me that was left, he had surrounded it and protected it with "iron and bronze" and left it in the "grass" of this field I'm in so it would grow again. God knew I would come back, and when I did – even though at this point in my life I'm still struggling – God knows how my story ends, and it's not over yet. And until it does, He's got me protected and surrounded in this jungle I've been dropped into, so that

8 Daniel 4:15 [NIV]

when I'm ready, and as I continue to grow in this grassy field of unknowns, I will come back.

Chapter 9

...and then there were three...

Friday, January 4th, 1964

My back is throbbing...it's midnight...I just want to sleep. Chuck's working a swing shift. He'll be home soon, and then we'll sleep. But there's no sleep for me tonight. The pain in my back is increasingly worse.

We're staying at my parent's house while Chuck was building our first home next door. I was standing in front of the heater blowing hot air; it seemed to help my back a little... for a few moments – then it would get worse again. I'd fallen earlier that day after mopping and waxing the kitchen floor to help my mom out. I was eight and a half months pregnant with our first child. Without thinking, I walked only a short distance across the freshly waxed floor before landing hard. I'm sure that's why my back was hurting.

Five o'clock in the morning on that little farm was early but it was "gettin'-up" time. There were cows to milk, and horses, pigs, and chickens to feed. A lot of work to be done.

I was glad I was pregnant; I didn't have to do any of that now. I'd grown up on this little farm with my parents, three brothers, and two sisters since I was 10 years old. I was second to the oldest. The four older ones knew what the "chores" of farm life looked like, and it wasn't easy. There were always animals to feed and care for, barns to clean, stalls to muck, hay to bale, gardens to plant, harvest, and then canning the foods.

Our food was mostly raised right there. Dad always told us, "Don't make pets with the animals, we'll eat them this winter." After my 4-H Blue Ribbon Prize winner, little lamb, I learned that tough lesson. Then another lesson I'd learned quickly was the little baby pig I'd chosen for my next 4-H entry. Gave her a bath, put a pink ribbon around her neck, and off to the County Fair we went. We came home with a Blue Ribbon; she was so cute. Turned her loose, and she went running straight for the biggest mud-hole in the pasture. Just goes to prove if the clean-up is only on the outside, the inside will run to the mud hole every time. We ate her that winter too.

By now, I needed a bullet to bite. My back pain had become moans and groans. My mom's footsteps echoed as she came down the hallway. She took one look at me and said, "Linda, you're in labor!" "Labor? No, No, I'm not. I've got three more weeks," I managed to moan out. I heard her head back down the hallway to our bedroom door and woke up Chuck telling him, "Linda's in labor. You need to get her to the hospital."

Have you ever recognized that when there's an emergency, the car is always low on gas? It's five o'clock in the morning, and we're fifteen miles from the hospital. Then to add to that, it's so foggy outside you could barely see. Chuck stopped at the first gas station we saw that was open to fill up. As I sat there waiting in the car, shivering from the cold

January weather, my back aching, I just wanted to go back home. Yeah that's what I'll tell Chuck when he gets back in the car. "Baby," I said as he was starting up the car, "let's go home and pretend this isn't happening." He looked at me, grinning from ear to ear, and said, "Sweetheart, there's about to be another baby in this household, and this baby is a tiny one, and there's no turning back now."

Arriving at the hospital we stopped at the registration desk. "No, we're not registered. She's not due for three weeks..." The sound of Chuck's voice as he spoke those words told me he wasn't playing games anymore. The girl looked at me and said, "Well, she's not going to make it three weeks." Within minutes I was whisked off in a wheelchair, leaving Chuck to finish paperwork. My nerves had now flipped over the edge, far from any calmness - had there been any since midnight. I thought...I'm not ready for this; where's Chuck? ... maybe I'll change my mind. I'll tell them I'm just going to go home. Yeah, that should work. Besides I'm not registered – right? It didn't work.

I was placed in a room with five other mothers in labor. Their moans, and screams now scared me spitless. One by one a couple of nurses would come and roll one of their beds out. All day long until it was only me left – alone. It's now almost ten hours later. I'd been given something to help me relax when I first came in, and at times, I'd drift off to sleep only to be awakened by this excruciating pain IN MY BACK! My doctor finally came in. He patted me on the hand and said, "Young lady, let's go. It's time for your little baby to face the world." It seemed to be just minutes and a few pushes, and then there it was, my baby's cry. I heard the doctor, as he went to the waiting room door, where all expectant fathers stayed, say, "Mr. Querry, (I found out later Chuck, like me, was the only dad left in that waiting room), you have a son." We named him Kevin.

The sound of baby cries at two o'clock in the morning gradually became normal around our home. Before long it was the pitter-patter of tiny feet, and our lives changed forever.

Chapter 10

tears, tears, & more tears

> **"** I hide my tears when I say your name,
> but the pain in my heart is still the same.
> Although I smile and seem carefree,
> there is no one who misses you
> . . . more than me! **"**
> **all-greatquotes.com**

Tonight, I cried – no, I sobbed! I was perfectly fine – and then I wasn't. Tears – they appear unexpectedly! They remind me of all the first memories and the last ones. Tears, like a waterfall over a dam, they flood my face. Like a wave that knocks me down when I think I've got my feet planted firmly. Like a gut-punch in the stomach that takes my breath away.

Tears, they come when I'm longing to feel your arms around me once more. They come when I'm missing your sweet, gentle kisses. They come when I wish, for just one more time, that I could smell the aroma of your cologne as that fragrance flowed through the house where you'd been.

Tears, they come when I'm walking into the mall, or a grocery store, or church, and I wish you were there to reach out and take my hand as we walked. You always took my hand – even when I was aggravated at you about something, you'd reach, I'd pull away, and you'd grab me and take my hand firmly in yours – and then everything would be okay.

Tears, they show up when I'm watching a movie. They are there when I'm facing a decision and need you to talk to. They're there when the car needs an oil change. They show up when the smoke alarm starts beeping, which is too high for me to reach.

Tears, they're there as I lay down alone in my bed at night knowing the warmth of your body lying next to me isn't there anymore. Tears, when I just want to lay my head on your chest and hear your heart beating again. Your heartbeat was so strong – until it wasn't.

Tears, they come a few drops at a time, they come like a faucet that I can't turn off. Sometimes they're silent as I choke them back, not allowing them to come out. Sometimes they're loud – they burst forth like a volcano eruption.

Tears show up on birthdays; yours, our kids, our grandchildren's, and our great's. Tears are there when another great-grandchild is born, knowing they will never know you or be bounced on your knee as you sing them one of your silly songs.

Tears are there because "we" "you-and-me we" can't celebrate our anniversaries together anymore. Tears show up on holidays. Tears are there at the ball games because you're not here with us celebrating the victories.

Today, as I write this, it's been five years and two months. Sixty-two months. Tears aren't here every day, but I still cry.

Tears help. Tears relieve the pressure of your absence that seems to build up inside my heart, waiting to explode. Tears, the sound of love with no place to go.

When the pain of this brokenness is so great it hurts, there'll be tears. I'll cry, weep, and even sob at times, and I won't be ashamed of my tears. They'll remind me that, one day, Jesus will wipe them all away. (Revelation 21:4 NIV) But until that day, I allow my tears.

> The moment that you left me,
> my heart was split in two;
> one side was filled with memories;
> the other side died with you.
>
> I often lay awake at night
> When the world is fast asleep;
> and take a walk down memory lane
> with tears upon my cheeks.
>
> Remembering you is easy,
> I do it every day;
> but missing you is a heartache
> that never goes away.
>
> I hold you tightly within my heart
> And there you will remain,
> You see, life has gone on without you,
> but will never be the same.
> **-author unknown**

Chapter 11

did I just throat-punch you?

"**G**etting over it so soon? But the words are ambiguous. To say the patient is getting over it after an operation for appendicitis is one thing; after he's had his leg off, is quite another. After that operation, either the wounded stump heals, or the man dies. If it heals, the fierce, continuous pain will stop. Presently he'll get back his strength and be able to stump about on his wooden leg. He has 'got over it.' But he will probably have recurrent pains in the stump all his life, and perhaps pretty bad ones; and he will always be a one-legged man. There will be hardly any moment when he forgets it. Bathing, dressing, sitting down, and getting up again, even lying in bed, will all be different. His whole way of life will be changed. All sorts of pleasures and activities that he once took for granted will have to be simply written off. Duties too. At present, I am learning to get about on crutches. Perhaps I shall presently be given a wooden leg. But I shall never be biped again."

-C.S. Lewis – excerpts from "A Grief Observed"

Wounded. Crippled. Unable to walk without help. Shock... just a few words that might describe me after losing the love of my life. People need to realize this isn't something you "get over."

I was standing after a convention (one year after my husband received his wings), talking with some close friends. As I shared what had happened, tears filled my eyes. About that time, a "friend" walked by, slapped me on the back, and said, "Honey, honey, it's been a year, get over it." I wanted to "throat punch" her. Seriously, did you just say that? And note, she had lost her husband two years earlier - one year before my husband.

As I gasped to get my breath, I turned away from the friends I was just talking to because I knew a gush of tears was about to explode out of my eyes. When I turned, there stood another friend, who is "family of choice," who'd lost his beautiful wife several years before. He motioned for me to come over to him. I shook my head no, mouthing the words, "I'm okay." I just needed to get out of there. He didn't take "no" for my answer and said, "Come here." I walked over to him, and without saying a word, he opened his arms and wrapped me up in them, and I wept. Within a few moments, the thought flashed through my brain that he was single. So I stood back, my face a wet mess of liquid, trying to apologize, saying, "I'll be alright." He assured me there was no apology necessary and that he would always be there for me (and he always was and still is if I need him). I thanked him and rushed to my car. Now a sobbing mess, I wanted to "throat punch" someone – anyone. As soon as I thought that, a flashback from the movie, "Steel Magnolias," flashing like a Neon sign, "...go ahead, hit HER, hit OUISER!" I just needed to find "Ouiser!"

So often, people trying to make you feel better, say the worst things. Like, "You'll be okay, you'll get over it," or "This is your chapter two," or "Just think, they're in a better place." Well of course they are, but I'm not! Or, "You'll see them again real soon." Wait! What? Should I be worried?

But the worst ever, someone told me recently that had been said to them, "Let me pray that grief demon out of you!" How about I just "throat punch" you? The Urban Dictionary defines a "throat punch" as "a rapid, unexpected knuckle thrust in the larynx of the one who is pissing you off, causing pain and discomfort." Well, thank you, Urban Dictionary!

Now, let me go on to say this, I have only "thought" that thought. I have yet to carry it out. (Smiles) I'm not a violent person and never would be. Nevertheless, people need to "pause and think" about what they are saying to someone who is trying to just get through the next 24-hour day, before they speak.

We're that person C.S. Lewis was referencing. We're crippled and maybe even gotten the wooden leg trying to figure out how to walk with it. Grief is an amputation of part of the heart. Split in two. Searching for ways to breathe normally again, to stand up straight and walk, and find our way "through" this new life we've been handed. Maybe when you see someone grieving, a hug could be much more meaningful than any words you can speak. "Let's go get coffee or tea, and we can chat or not, but I'm here for you. . ." is the best thing that you can do. So many times, because our loss makes people feel uncomfortable, it's easier to just stay away from us. But that's the worst thing you can do! We're already battling abandonment. Don't you abandon us too. We need you in our lives. We're crippled, trying to heal something we'll never get over.

I love the song Willie Nelson sings:

"Something You Get Through."
When you lose the one you love
You think your world has ended
You think your world will be a waste of time
Without them in it.
You feel there's no way to go on

Life is just a sad, sad song.
But love is bigger than us all
The end is not the end at all.
It's not somethin' you get over
But it's somethin' you get through
It's not ours to be taken
It's just a thing we get to do.

Life goes on and on
And when it's gone
It lives in someone new
It's not something you get over
But it's something you get through.[9]

It's just something you get "through" ... not over, ever! It's that tunnel of darkness like a train is about to enter, that curves around and you can't see the light at the end. You don't bail off the train, you trust that the conductor knows

9 Written by: BUDDY CANNON, WILLIE NELSON; Lyrics © BMG Rights Management, Sony/ ATV Music Publishing LLC, released 2018 on the album: Last Man Standing

there is a light at the end. I have learned that no matter how dark it seems, I can trust my Conductor, I can trust God, because He's promised *"He will never leave me, or forsake me"* in this dark tunnel or anywhere else.

Chapter 12

footsteps into unknown paths

March 5th, 1965

T he U-Haul was loaded. Snow was predicted. The good-byes were tearful. We were about to head off three-hours away from my hometown, Eugene, to Madras, a tiny little town in Central Oregon to pastor our first church.

That first Sunday afternoon, October 1962, when I met Chuck, my friend invited him to church that night. He went. After the sermon that night, the altar call was given, and several people went forward and knelt at the altar. I went to the altar, and that night I was praying for Chuck. That can of beer, which was sitting on the floor next to his chair that afternoon, scared me, but the feelings I had felt made me believe there was a connection. I had already planned to break it off with the guy I'd gotten together with on that blind date that Sunday night. I'd been praying the past couple of weeks, "God, I'm done dating, until You Lord, bring into my path, the man You want me to marry." As the Pastor was about to close the altar call, I got up to return to my seat. That's when I saw Chuck, who had been seated on the back row, beside the guy I was dating, (who was his best friend - and drinking buddy - which I did not know), get up and not walk to the altar, he ran to the altar. Chuck totally surrendered his life to God. He told me later that he'd get paid on Friday night, head to the bar with his buddy, and they'd drink all weekend until their whole paycheck was gone by Monday morning. I've heard him say so many times, "I was one weekend away from being an alcoholic." After that night, Chuck never drank again. God had completely delivered him from alcohol.

We started dating two weeks later, after a youth roller skating party. My friend Faye and I literally taught Chuck how to roller skate. There were a lot of "pick-ups" that night, and it wasn't his "lines." (LOL)

Now here we were, about to begin a journey, and we had no idea where this road would lead us.

It had been about a year earlier after returning home from church one Sunday night, we'd just laid down in bed. We had spent an hour taking turns, bouncing our two-month-old son, Kevin, up and down that night, trying to get him to sleep after battling another colicky night. Lying there, both of us facing the ceiling, just talking and laughing at the joys – the ups and the downs - of parenthood. When Chuck, now with a very serious tone in his voice said, "There's something I want to ask you." "Okay," I said, not sure why our conversation now sounded so serious. "How would you feel about being a Pastor's wife?" he asked. I sat straight up in bed and squealed, in my soft tiny squeal to keep from waking Kevin, who was finally sleeping soundly in the cradle next to us. "A Pastor's wife? Are you serious?" I turned to look at him and could barely see the reflection of his face in the darkness. "Are you serious? Seriously, are you serious?" I tried to keep my voice low, but the excitement in my whole body made it hard to do. Chuck smiled that smile that could make my heart skip beats, and continued, "Yes, I'm serious. I've been running from this since I was a teenager. I enlisted in the Navy and spent four years trying to drown it out of my head. I'm tired of running. I can't run anymore."

Faye, my Pastor's daughter, and my best friend, who'd introduced us, had invited me to their home so many times. Every time I'd be in her home and watch her parents, I'd dream of the day that I could be a Pastor's wife – just relaxing on a Sunday afternoon, no cows to milk, no pigs to slop (it's a southern slang I'm sure), no chores! I never had a clue until this night that that was even possible.

Chuck was the Superintendent of the Sunday School at our church and the Worship Leader, but he'd never even spoken of or given me a hint that he would ever, or even wanted to be, a Pastor. My heart was about to explode! I wanted to get up and jump on the bed. Scream out loud, – I'm going to be Pastor's wife! I'M GOING TO BE A PASTOR'S WIFE!!!! YES, a Pastor's wife. Chuck quickly settled me down, pointing to the cradle where our little one was still ASLEEP as he put his finger over my lips whispering, "sssshhh." We talked. Chuck talked. I talked. We talked and talked that night, living "our" dream life before it ever started - until he fell asleep.

Now, after a year of Chuck's preparation for ministry, and getting his first Minister's License, that dream was becoming a reality. I'd never been far from my parents and friends, but the excitement within me outweighed the sadness of leaving,

Mom held on tightly to her first and only grandchild Kevin, now 14 months old. The pitter-patter of his little feet at Grandma's house wouldn't be heard every day now. Our house next door had been finished, but now rented to unknown strangers, would be a reminder to my mom that her grandchild didn't live there anymore. The hardest thing that morning was taking Kevin from my mom's arms as tears streamed down her face.

I grew up with very, very few hugs, and the phrase "I love you" wasn't a part of our lives. All that changed shortly after I married Chuck. He taught me the importance of saying "I love you," and his family was the hugging-ness people I'd ever been around. They'd leave to go to the grocery store and hug you when they left and then hug you again when they came home...and no, that's not an exaggeration. (smiles) I loved those hugs, but it was still so hard for me to give them without feeling uncomfortable.

This morning, as hard as it was, I'd taken Kevin, and put him in the car seat in the car. Just a note, car seats in those days were metal, and any child could unsnap and lift the brace in front of them and climb out or climb over them. After he was "secured" in the car seat, I went back and for a moment, hugged and held my mom in my arms as she wept.

In a few moments, Chuck and my Dad pulled out in the U-Haul; I followed in the car behind them. As we headed across the mountain, the snow started falling. Snow scared me. Chuck had told me before we left that if we hit snow, don't stop, just keep going, or you'll get stuck. That frightened me even more. I had a 14-month-old baby in the car. I couldn't afford to get stuck or stranded in the snow. As we were going up the steepest part of the Santiam/McKenzie Pass, with the snow falling heavily now, the U-Haul started slowing down. Not sure of what I should do, or what was happening, I followed. I watched as Chuck did what he told me not to do – stop! I pulled as close to the snowbank as possible and stopped behind them, unsure of what was happening.

My Dad was a mechanic, and a very good one. In fact, that's why we moved from North Carolina to Eugene, Oregon in 1955. He'd been offered a Head Mechanic position at the Ford Motor Company, making five times the money he was making in North Carolina. I watched as my dad lifted the hood of that U-Haul. I felt a little better knowing my Dad was with us, but I knew now, something was wrong, and it was snowing hard. After a few minutes Chuck walked back to the car. I rolled the window down, the cold of the falling snow hit me in the face. "Brrr," I said, "What's wrong?" Chuck assured me Dad was going to fix it but he needed a "paper clip." "A paper clip?" I questioned, "Where am I going to find a paper clip?" I searched through my purse, through the diaper bag-as if I'd have a paper clip in the diaper bag? Nothing found. The cold snow now blowing in the car window caused a shiver up my spine. I looked through the glove compartment. Nothing. I took the bag of snacks that was sitting on the floorboard of the passenger seat and searched. Kevin, now sitting "secured" in his "car seat" in the "front seat" (yeah-things have changed) saw the Cheerios and reached for some. I lifted the box out of the bag of snacks I'd purchased the day before, and there under that box – was – WAIT for it - a paper-clip! I handed the paper clip to Chuck, stunned, wondering how did a paper clip end up in that bag? And how was a paper clip the solution to that U-Haul problem? If you believe that God goes before you, then I'm sure now you're shaking your head saying as I did, "Thank you Lord, only You would know we would need a paper clip!"

Within minutes, the U-Haul started and was attempting to pull out. Spinning wheels throwing snow in my windshield. I knew we were stuck. I tried to move forward to no avail. The U-Haul tires were spinning, my car tires were spinning. I didn't know what to do, and here we are stuck on the side of a mountain. When what to my wondering eyes did appear, a snowplow coming up that mountain. Splashing snow all over my side window, he stopped beside the driver's door of the U-Haul. Within a minute, Chuck put his arm out of the window and motioned for me to follow him. We both pulled out, spinning, slipping and sliding until we were behind and in the snowplow's tracks. We followed behind that snowplow, in his tracks the rest of the way across that mountain.

Arriving at our destination, when my Dad and Chuck returned the U-Haul, the man could not believe that a "paper clip" had held that part in that U-Haul together as we traveled across that mountain and the other hour and half to our new home. I don't remember what the "part" was, but I never forgot that part of our journey. But God!

That was just the beginning of miracles that started our footsteps into unknown paths to ministry at that first little church.

Chapter 13

and then there were four...

"Trusting God in the Storm...with small miracles along the way."

August, 1966

Chuck had left a good paying Supervising job when we accepted the pastoral role of ministry. In fact, his boss said to him when he told him he was leaving, "Are you crazy? You're quitting a good job to go be a preacher without a salary?" My dad said pretty much the same words. Someone once said, "Faith is trusting God in the middle of the storm." That first pastorate taught us to trust God in the storms.

Some people use the phrase "broke, busted, and disgusted," and even though we were very familiar with that phrase, there was never a time when we ever thought or talked about turning back. It was the blessings from God that we were thankful for. Those blessings and lots of miracles along the way got us through the tough times.

There were eight of us in church that first Sunday morning in March of 1965. There wasn't a paycheck coming any time soon. Chuck had been to the unemployment office several times, but nothing happened.

One afternoon a knock came on our door. It was the "Supervisor," the man in charge at the Unemployment Office. He asked Chuck as he opened the door, "Are you Charles Querry? Do you still want a job?" Who does that? When was the last time you had someone from a job site or an unemployment office knock on your door? Things were "picking up!" Chuck was a carpenter and a very good one. He went to work the next morning with the Sanitation department – riding on the back of a garbage truck, "picking up" cans of garbage. (smiles) One thing I learned quickly about my husband that day was that there wasn't a job of any kind that he wouldn't accept to take care of his family.

But the miracles didn't end there. Before Chuck got his first paycheck, we didn't have the money, and our car payment of $92.78 was due. That was a big payment, for 1965, on our new 1965 Ford Fairlane car, which we purchased with a loan for $3,000. (I know - wow!) I went to the mailbox one day, and there was a letter from Chuck's niece – his brother's daughter, Wanda. In the letter, she wrote, "I was praying and I felt like God spoke to me to send you my tithes..." The amount of the check was – are you ready for it - $92.78! The exact amount of our car payment. Wow again! But God!

Oh, but there's more. Our ladies' group at church – uh, let me think – there were four of us. We were making "fried pies" to sell to help with the building fund for a new church. From the beginning, we were renting a large two-story house. Half of it was the Sanctuary for church, and the other half was where we lived. Our little church had grown beyond the size of that half of the house. One year later, Chuck was building the new church in his "spare" time. Let me pause long enough to bring you up to this day.

Times were tough for everyone, and money was scarce. The renters had moved out of our house in Eugene and caused a lot of damage. There was work to be done before we could rent it again, and it was a huge part of our income. We were expecting our second baby any day. We had waited and waited and waited. The baby was due on August 1st, and it was now three weeks later. My last doctor's appointment had shown, per the doctor, I wasn't anywhere near a delivery date. (No ultrasounds were available in 1966 to pinpoint a delivery date). So, Friday, when Chuck got off work, he jumped in the car and headed three hours away to Eugene to make the necessary repairs and get our house rented again. My Mom took a Greyhound bus from Eugene to come to stay with me.

It was the following Tuesday morning in August 1966; it was hot, and I couldn't sleep. I woke up with that excruciating pain in my back. This time I knew it was labor. There wasn't a slow progression; the pain seemed unbearable from the beginning. My mom didn't drive, so I called a lady from church and asked her if she'd drive me to the hospital – 30 minutes away, in Redmond. When we arrived, it wasn't long before the doctor told me my baby was breech. The pain was horrific by this time. The doctor explained to me he was going to try and turn the baby. Turn the baby? That seemed impossible to me. I begged for something for the pain. He told me he couldn't give me anything for the pain because he needed the baby's help in the turning, and any medication would also medicate the baby. The turning process was underway, the pain was the worst imagined, and I needed a bullet to bite – no, I needed to push – just one time let me P U S H; I couldn't stop. At that point, the doctor screamed at me, "If you push, you're going to break this baby's neck!" As if I wasn't already scared, this frightened me even more. My mom was standing by me. I just wanted Chuck. I needed Chuck, who was now on that three-hour trip back to Redmond from Eugene.

Time seemed to be moving in slow motion. I felt like I was passing out, as if I was hovering over this scene, watching everything. I heard the doctor say to my mom, "I can't save them both, it has to be the baby or her." My mom's words seemed to echo in that room when she said, "Save my daughter." At that point, I struggled to just speak, and I screamed with every ounce of breath in me, "NO! SAVE MY BABY!" I could barely hear the doctor as he talked to himself, "Come on, little one, work with me." I could hear my mom praying. I could feel myself as if I was drifting farther and farther away from them all. Then the doctor screamed at me again, "PUSH, Linda, PUSH! PUSH NOWWWW!" Finally, I PUSHED! Then, there it was. The sound of my screaming baby brought me back into that hospital room. "You have a beautiful son," he said, as he laid him on my tummy. I looked up at my mom, now crying, saying, "It's all okay now; it's all okay."

A few hours later, I heard the doctor outside my room as he spoke to my husband. "I'm glad you're finally here," he said harshly, "we almost lost them both!" (Just FYI, that doctor missed the "bedside manners" class in Med school).

Chuck walked into my room in tears. As he held me and his newborn son, he kept saying, "I'm so sorry, I'm so sorry. I shouldn't have left." But the apologies turned to smiles before long. How could you not smile, looking into the tiny, little baby blue eyes of our second son, now named Randy.

A few hours before, all looked hopeless; now I was staring into the face of another miracle. But God!

Now back to continue from the "pause" earlier.

Randy was a few weeks old. A two-year-old, a newborn, formula, doctor bills - money was even tighter or none at all. Chuck had had another "house call" from the man at the unemployment office offering him a better job - driving a truck delivering lumber to building sites. But we hadn't gotten his first paycheck yet. The only food in the house was one small can of Similac formula and half a bag of potatoes.

We lived in "potato" country. When our church members received their paychecks working at the potato factory, their job gave them a bag of potatoes. They tithed us with 10-lb bags of potatoes. I learned to make potato soup, potato pancakes, mashed potatoes, fried potatoes, hash-brown potatoes, potatoes all rotten – uh, sorry, I mean au-gratin. Potatoes were many times the only thing on our table, but we were thankful. Now even the potatoes were almost gone.

It was a Saturday morning; Chuck was working on the church property site, building the new church. I was at one of the ladies' trailer homes, making fried pies with the three other ladies. It was late in the afternoon when we finished making and delivering the pies. Exhausted, I took Kevin and Randy and headed home. When I went into the kitchen, I opened the refrigerator to get a bottle for Randy. I stood there, shocked. The refrigerator was packed. There wasn't an inch without something in it. I opened the freezer above, and it was packed from top to bottom with meats. I shut the door, thinking my brain was playing tricks on me, and opened it again. I touched the milk; it wasn't a figment of my imagination. It was real. I walked over to the cupboards where groceries were kept when we had some. From the top to the bottom, those four shelves were full. By now, tears are flowing. Within a few moments, Chuck came home. I said, "Babe, come look!" I opened the refrigerator, then the cabinet. His face was as shocked as mine had been, as he asked, "Where did you get the money? Where did this come from?" Lifting my arms with a shrug of my shoulders, I told him nobody gave me money; I didn't buy any of this.

Doors were never locked in those days. After asking some of our church members if they'd done it, and they hadn't, we had no clue where those groceries came from. It was three months later that we got a call from Chuck's sister, Patsy, and she told us the story. She and her husband, Jerry, were going on vacation (they lived four hours away on the Oregon coast). She said they were driving close by and decided to come visit for a while. When they got there, nobody was home, so they decided to fix themselves a sandwich and then go on to their vacation destination. She went on to explain when they opened the fridge and there was no food, and also no food in the cupboards, they decided to take their vacation money and fill our kitchen with food... then they went back home. Who does that? But God!

...the small miracles along the way.

I never questioned why God had sent us to that "desert" place for our first pastorate. It taught us to trust God in the storms, regardless of where we were. It taught us that in the deepest, darkest moments in our lives, nothing was ever a surprise to God. God didn't wake up one morning and put His hands over His face and exclaim, "Oh my goodness, how did this happen?" The psalmist wrote in Psalms 121:3-4:

> "He [God] will not let your foot be moved; He who keeps you will not slumber. Behold, He who keeps (Israel) *[insert your name there]* will neither slumber or sleep."

God isn't snoozing while you're in a storm. There's a miracle walking on your stormy waters or your snowy mountains.

• • • • • • • • • • • • • • •

A few days before my husband went home to be with the Lord, my son, Kevin, got a phone call from a former State Overseer of ours, Bishop Mark Williams. Mark had become much more than our Overseer; he'd become a true family friend. He preached in our church numerous times during the ten years we were pastoring in Las Vegas, Nevada. He was there in family crises to help our family through it. On that phone call that day, June 10, 2017, he told Kevin to tell his Dad to "expect small miracle along the way."

Chuck had been out for hours at a time and had done very little talking for several days. The hospital had him on pain meds, so he slept a lot. Kevin came back into the room, leaned over his Dad's bed, and whispered in his ear the words Bishop Mark had told him. From that conversation, Chuck immediately woke up and began talking about how much he loved Bishop Mark. We called Randy, who was still in the parking lot after visiting his Dad, to come back, and Facetimed Rodney in Illinois. Then Chuck spoke to each of his sons and our one grandson, Daniel, who was there that day. He began telling them how proud he was of them. He looked at me and told me he loved me, and then looked above my head with a smile on his face I'd never seen. I asked, "Babe, what are you looking at?" His reply was, "There ain't nothing bad up here. It's joy unspeakable; it's so beautiful."

Then he wanted to sing that hymn, "Amazing Grace." When we finished the song, he closed his eyes, and he was out of it again. I thought he was gone. He wasn't. Early that evening, he was transferred to a Nursing Facility. Every time I'd walk in his room and ask, "How are you, Babe?", His answer was ALWAYS, "Oh, sweetheart, it's so beautiful here." It wasn't beautiful there in that room. The man in the bed beside him used foul, offensive, vulgar language constantly, screamed every time we prayed, or if we had more people in the room than he thought should be there, he'd call the Supervisor in.

After the third day, when I went in and asked Chuck how he was, and he said, "Oh, sweetheart, it's so beautiful here," I took his face in my hands and looked him in the eyes, and said, "Listen to me, sweetheart. I'm sorry Babe, but It's NOT beautiful in here!" He looked straight into my eyes and said, "Can't you see it, Linda? It's beautiful here." No, I couldn't see what he was seeing. But that day I was reminded of Bishop Mark's words, "Expect small miracles along the way." I truly believe that when Chuck was awake, he knew anyone and everyone who came to visit with him, up to the last night; but when he closed his eyes he was in heaven.

Because of all those "big" miracles God brought to pass early in our lives, it made it easier for me to believe those eleven days prior to Chuck's departure to heaven, were the "small miracles along the way."

People ask me all the time, "What did you and Chuck talk about when you found out he was terminal, when the cancer diagnosis only gave him six months. Did you talk about him dying?" My answer was always, "NO!" Not ever, not once, did we talk about him dying. You see, every morning as I'd walk into that hospital room or that Nursing Facility,

I'd think, "This is the day he will be healed; he will get his miracle! He'll be sitting up on the side of the bed saying, 'Get my clothes!' And then he'd say, just like he did fifty-four years ago when we were pronounced husband and wife, 'Let's get out of here!'"

But that's not what happened. My miracle prayer was to see him completely healed, completely whole, completely well, and the active man I knew three months earlier, and we'd walk out of the facility hand in hand with a great testimony for the world to hear. But God's way, God's thoughts, so much higher than mine, had a better miracle for Charles Querry. God wanted him back in heaven, healed, well, and whole.

I know my mind has crazy, wild thoughts at times. So, with that in mind, and if you're reading this, neither you nor I have been to heaven, so maybe, just maybe, God needed another good carpenter to finish building my mansion, and He knew Chuck would know exactly what I liked. Maybe he needed a good strong voice to lead a choir of angels singing, "How Great Thou Art," or maybe, just maybe, the book God wrote about Charles Querry seventy-nine and half years ago, was completed.

You see, I'm living the miracle now; I've made it this far until I finish the book God wrote about me.

" One day you'll tell your story of how you've overcome what you're going through now, and it will become part of someone else's survival guide. **"**

- @brightvibes.com

Chapter 14

broken-heart syndrome

If you're walking this journey of losing your soulmate, your true love, your best friend, then I'm sure, like me, you've faced days that you think you won't survive or even want to.

Six months after my husband left this old world for his eternal home, I ended up in the Emergency Room with heart attack symptoms. Within an hour, I had been admitted. Three days later and after running numerous tests, the Cardiologist Doctor came into my room and said, "I've ran every test possible and everything comes back negative." Then he asked me, "What is causing your stress?" Hmmm, let me think - my husband of 54 years just left me for heaven.

Hearing me explain this, his next words shook me. "Have you ever known someone who lost their companion and a few weeks or a few months later they passed away also?" I replied yes. He said, "Most of the time they die from 'Broken Heart Syndrome.'" He went on to say, "I haven't lost my wife, so I can't tell you how long this kind of grief lasts. But I will tell you this, after all your tests, including searching for any cancer, and every test came back negative, you are suffering from 'Broken Heart Syndrome.' I can't tell you when you won't cry anymore. I can't tell you when the hurt ends, if ever, but I can tell you that unless you find a reason to keep living, this will take your life also."

Those words shook me. I glanced over at my son, Kevin, who was sitting with me, and I could see it shook him too. After the doctor left the room, Kevin said to me, "Mom, it's been awful losing Pop, but do you want to add to our pain if we lose you too?"

I left the hospital that next day. For the next 17 months I continued having chest pressure, my left arm aching, nothing was getting better. I started having stomach attacks, like gallbladder attacks, except I didn't have a gallbladder anymore. I was only able to eat Jell-O and applesauce for months without one of those attacks. I knew something was wrong, but I kept hearing the doctor's words, "your tests are all negative... Broken-Heart Syndrome..." So why go to the doctor? I had been diagnosed.

I had a church business meeting scheduled, that I was conducting on a Friday night in September 2019. I had been gradually getting weaker the whole week. I tried to just have enough energy to get in the shower and get ready, but there was no energy left in me. I called my bookkeeper (and a very special friend, Brandy) to ask her to pick up the pies I was supposed to get and I would meet her at 6:00pm for the meeting. Her response was, "I'm coming over, you don't sound good." "No," I said, "just pick up the pies and meet me at church at 6:00pm." She didn't listen. Within minutes a knock came on my door, and I opened it to find both her and her husband standing there. It was all I could do to have the energy to walk back to my chair. Again, I told them both, "I'll be okay, go pick up the pies, I'll get in the shower, get dressed and meet you at the church as planned." I was talking to deaf ears.

Against my wishes, they called the paramedics. As the paramedic squatted down in front of me, he looked at me after asking me several questions and said, "We're taking you to the Emergency Room tonight." I responded, using every bit of strength I could muster, and said, "Oh no, you can't do that, I have a business meeting I have to conduct tonight." His face moved closer to mine, his eyes now spot on with my eyes and said, "You're not doing a business meeting tonight, you're going to the Emergency Room!" Again, I responded with, "You don't understand, I'm conducting the business meeting. I am the Pastor! I HAVE to be there!" Again, his face moved closer to mine and with our eyes glaring at each other again, he said, "Do you see that bed over there?" pointing to the gurney they'd now positioned at the doorway of my apartment. "Either you're going to walk over to it, or I'm going to carry you over there, and I don't care if you're the President, you're NOT going to a business meeting tonight!" Before you think it, yes, I've been called "stubborn" and "hard-headed" before. (smiles)

I don't remember walking to that gurney, and I don't remember the ambulance ride to the hospital that night. I do remember sitting there, so sick, with my very dear friend, (who literally saved my life that night), saying to her, "We've got to get out of here, I've got a business meeting to do." Little did I know, the Emergency Room doctor was close enough to hear me say that. She came over and was right in my face and said, "Listen to me, you're not going anywhere but to surgery tonight or you'll be gone by morning." Whoa! What? Gone?

I didn't go to the meeting that night, I also didn't go to surgery that night. My vitals were dangerously low. I didn't go on Saturday either for the same reasons. They had me drinking horrible tasting stuff. I had no potassium, no iron, no Vitamin K no.... the lists were endless. Late Saturday night a doctor came into my room and said, "You're going to surgery in the morning, first thing." I said, "It's Sunday!" But hey, I refrained from saying I need to be in church, I'm the Pastor. He looked at me and said sternly, "Young lady," (that made me feel a little better), "it doesn't matter that it's Sunday, you're lucky to be alive. If you had waited another twenty-four hours, you would have been dead! So, whether or not your vitals are up where they should be, you're going to surgery first thing in the morning, and we're going to try to save your life." Needless to say, I didn't sleep much that night. I was drinking Vitamin K (ugh) and whatever concoction they'd bring me every hour, plus non-stop blood draws.

I did go to surgery. As they were preparing me for surgery, the nurse asked me, "Honey, do you have family waiting in the waiting room?" "No," I replied. I didn't tell her my three sons were in Dallas, Texas at a Dallas Cowboys football game – a gift they'd given each other. I'd assured them that I would be okay. (I know you just rolled your eyes). She then asked me, "Then do you have friends waiting?" again, I replied, "No." It was Sunday morning, all my friends were in church. (Another eye-roll? Really? LOL) At that point, this sweet precious nurse came around to the side of my bed, took my hand and asked, "Can I pray for you?" I replied enthusiastically, "YES, please do." She prayed a beautiful prayer over me and assured me she would be right beside me throughout the surgery. Sometimes I wonder, was that an angel, sent from heaven?

They removed a huge blockage in my bile duct. I found out later that blockage was causing my liver, my pancreas and my kidneys to shut down. As soon as I woke up after surgery, I knew I was better. It had been months since I felt good. I also knew I was going to keep getting better physically, and somehow, I was going to get through this journey of grief.

I've said it! I've posted it on social media! I've tried to get friends to understand it! Grief is REAL! HeartPAIN! It takes your breath away until you feel like you'll never get a deep breath again. It causes your chest to feel like an elephant is sitting on it. There's no time limit on it for you or me. Grief pain makes you SCREAM because something inside you hurts so badly you can't do anything else. Grief makes you walk fast to try and catch that person you just saw at the grocery store you were sure looked just like your soulmate. It unleashes liters of tears when you open the medicine cabinet, and there is his half bottle of cologne that you no longer smell the aroma as he walks by you. Grief made me leave a half bottle of water on his side of the bed's nightstand for three years because that was the last time he drank from it. Grief causes you to hang on to a key ring full of keys that you have no idea what they unlock anymore. Grief makes you hang on to a smooth stone he always carried in his pocket because he'd rub that stone when he was getting stressed over something. Grief makes you keep a used nail file because he used it the last time when he filed his nails. Grief causes you to leave the loose change he had in his pockets laying on the dresser, in the exact place he laid it the last time he changed clothes. Grief makes you keep a brand-new jar of black shoe wax you'd picked up for him because he needed to polish his shoes for Sunday – the last Sunday he did his sermon at church, while sitting on a stool because of the pain in his legs. Grief makes you question, "Why?" Why is that old man down the street, struggling and barely able to walk with a cane, still here, and my strong, active, and healthy husband gone? ...and the heartPAIN hurts more.

It's real pain! Just when you think it's gone forever, it comes back as you look at his watch on the dresser, and it stopped working at the exact time he died. The heartPAIN comes back, and it comes with a vengeance at times and crushes you to the floor in tears. Grief causes your "courage tank" to spring a leak, and fear entraps you at even the smallest tasks.

• • • • • • • • • • • • • • •

So how do we survive "Broken-Heart Syndrome?" The only way I've made it this far is by living it "One day at a time"! as my dear friend Bobby told me time and time again after losing his wife. That may sound almost like a cliché, but it's the only way I've made it these past five plus years. And some days it's one minute or one hour at a time. But if I try to figure out tomorrow, I'll crash and burn every time.

Grief is a sadness that holds my whole-body captive, imprisoned without parole. It burns, it aches, and it permeates every layer of my being. Even though I may briefly get a reprieve, it lingers near, ready to pounce on me as I enter my house alone or smell the flavor of a food that was his favorite.

I once ordered a salad that came with "diced" cucumbers mixed in it – just the way he liked his salad, and I choked back the tears because he wasn't there with me to enjoy it. How do you ever learn to handle the memories that trigger the grief to resurfaces again? I'm not sure you ever do!

I journal every week on the day he died. Those weeks turned into months. Those months turned to seasons – summer – fall – winter – spring. Then those months became holidays, birthdays, and anniversaries, that he wouldn't be a part of: births of grandchildren or great-grandkids that will never know what it's like for him to bounce them on his knee, and sing one of his silly "made-up" songs, that would make them giggle. They will only know him now through our stories. And we must keep telling them the stories, lest we forget. I won't forget. As hard as it is to experience the grief triggered by memories, I refuse to forget. Those journals help me remember. They hold my inmost secret feelings and how I've dealt with this thing called grief. Those journals are the expressions of my feelings that only I can fully grasp.

Days come, and days go, and I keep pushing myself to keep going. My life feels like I'm one of those American Ninja Warriors. I run! I jump! I grab hold of the next challenge in front of me. I fall! I shake it off. I get back up and the next time, I'll do it all over again. But as I climb the highest wall – the one that looks like it'll take me down – and I reach the top and RING that bell, I'll shout for the victory I've just accomplished. I'll raise my hands in the air, and jump up and down screaming, "Yeah! Yeah! I did it! I made it through that time!" ... and then I'll do it all over again the next time.

The one thing that keeps me going is that I remind myself over and over again that there's a reason God has me here.

My family needs me. My friends want me here. And hopefully through this book I'll be able to help others on this journey to deal with stuff nobody ever told us we'd face, and you'll make it too; the "BrokenHeart Syndrome" won't break you.

I hope this helps you today:

"I Never Went Away"

I stood by your bed last night;
I came to have a peep.
I could see that you were crying;
you found it hard to sleep.

I spoke to you softly
as you brushed away a tear,
"It's me, I haven't left you,
I'm well, I'm fine, I'm here."

I was close to you at breakfast,
I watched you pour the tea,
You were thinking of the many things,
and memories of me.

I was with you at the shops today;
your arms were getting sore.
I longed to take your parcels,
I wish I could do more.

I was with you at my grave today;
you tend it with such care.
I want to re-assure you,
that I'm not lying there.

I walked with you towards the house,
as you fumbled for your key.
I gently put my hand on you;
I smiled and said, "it's me."

You looked so very tired,
and sank into a chair.
I tried so hard to let you know,
that I was standing there.

It's possible for me,
to be so near you every day.
To say to you with certainty,
"I never went away."

You sat there very quietly,
then smiled, I think you knew...
in the stillness of that evening,
I was very close to you.

The day is over... I smile
and watch you yawning
and say "good-night, God bless,
I'll see you in the morning."

And when the time is right for you
to cross the brief divide,
I'll rush across to greet you
and we'll stand, side by side.

grief...how long will you linger here?

I have so many things to show you,
there is so much for you to see.
Be patient, live your journey out...
then come home to me.
- Author Unknown

Chapter 15

and then there were five...

when God goes before you . . .

Those roads of ministry led us from Oregon to Idaho, to California, to Colorado, to Illinois, and back to California. We took small churches to make them better. We accepted large churches that made us better. Our main goal was to enlarge the Kingdom of God – where we did, it was up to the Lord to lead us there. We've been ridiculed for moving around so much by people and by pastors, but to know in our hearts that every move was ordained of God has been our greatest satisfaction.

We had resigned from our church in Reedsport, on the Oregon coast, to accept the position of the Oregon State Youth Director. Our sons were four and two years old. So many memories...good, bad, and funny were made during our pastorates.

Kevin, our now almost four-year-old, decided one afternoon he could ride the little tricycle down the stairs of the house from the top to the bottom. We heard him when he hit the door at the bottom of the stairs. Untangling him from the trike and assuring him he was okay was followed by hilarious laughter. Kevin's biking adventurous continued. A few years later, at thirteen years old, while riding his brother Randy's Honda 50, his lack of attention gave him a jolt. As he passed us standing on the driveway watching, he looked at us and started waving madly, only to run into the pickup truck with a camper parked on the side of the street. We were thankful he had on a helmet that protected him while his head was banging back and forth on the pickup camper while the Honda 50 was still trying to proceed forward.

I'm sure some of you can identify with the fact that people thought a pastor and his family should always be poor. We never believed that and tried during our ministry for people to see what the Bible said, *"Beloved, I pray that you may prosper and be in health, just as our soul prospers."* (3 John 1:2 NKJV) Nevertheless, we didn't flaunt new clothes or things. Our second son, Randy, almost two years old now, was always wearing his older brother's "hand-me-down" clothes because they were still good clothes, just that Kevin had outgrown them. This particular time we had bought Randy a brand-new pair of shoes. He was so excited. We put them on him for Sunday morning church. He was so excited he said, "You mean I get to wear them first?" As we were getting him ready, I told him, "Randy, I don't want you to tell anyone you got new shoes." He shook his head in agreement with his little mischievous eyes twinkling. Again, I reiterated those words not to tell anyone. Since I played the piano for our services, both boys sat together on the front pew at church. I was playing prior to our service starting, and people were coming by to shake hands with my two little guys, all dressed up in their little suits. As people would greet them, Randy, with his little legs sticking straight out, would shake his feet back and forth until someone would notice and say, "Did you get new shoes?" Randy would tuck his chin and smile from ear to ear, nodding his head "yes" and then look at me with a look as if he was saying, "I didn't tell them."

The church in Reedsport was bigger than our first one but had tons of bills. Chuck went to work, not only to pay our bills, but we also paid the church bills. He would never allow church bills to go unpaid. There were times when I'd get so angry because we had no money because of that. I was troubled by a lot of things, disgruntled people in church, trying to make ends meet, taking care of two little ones and doctor appointments for them, and I felt sick physically. Everything just seemed to be piling up.

One afternoon I had just finished an all-day project of cleaning the house, washing windows, doing laundry, and corralling two toddlers, as Chuck came in from work. When he opened the door to enter through the living room, I said pretty strongly, "Take off your boots. I've cleaned house all day long!" His response as he was leaning over, untying his boots, he pointed to the corner behind me and said, smirkingly, "Well, you're not done. You didn't get those cobwebs up there behind you!" That did it! I was done! I shouted back at him, "I'm done! I'm done with everything! I'm done with these people! I'm done with you! I'm going to pack my bags, and I'm leaving!" He stood up, set his boots to the side, then placed his hands dramatically and firmly on his hips and said strongly, "And do you know what I'm going do?" "What?" I snapped back. With both hands on his hips and sticking his head out toward me, he responded, "I'm going to pack my bags and I'm going with you!" as he bolted across the living room floor, grabbing me up in his arms. I was struggling to get away, wrestling me to the floor as he's kissing my face all over. With my struggling and saying, "Remember, I'm mad!" He would respond, "Yeah, I am too!" Until we were both lying there on the floor laughing hysterically. That was the last time I threatened to leave him.

While to assume our State Youth Director position, we moved in with Chuck's sister. Our General Assembly for our church was a couple months away, and after the Assembly we would come back and take the Youth position. I took a job at a hospital, folding sheets and towels all day. It wasn't my dream job, but it gave us a little extra money for the trip to the General Assembly. Stressed, still feeling sick, struggling with our lives, juggling babysitting between our kids and Chuck's sister's kids, and where we were going, everything was just hard – but little did I know it was about to get harder.

I was constantly sick. So, trying to get better before our trip, I decided to go to the doctor. We didn't have insurance in those days, and that meant we would have to pay whatever it cost. I sat there on the bed in that doctor's office that day, with my head splitting, waiting for her to come back with test results. I had had headaches now for weeks. She finally walked in, smirking, and said, "You're going to have a baby! You're pregnant!" "Pregnant?" I replied with a huge question mark! "I can't be pregnant; I'm taking the birth control pill!" "Well," she said, "you're a part of the small percentage that it didn't work this time. So, stop taking the pill." I left that office that day so overwhelmed I didn't know what to do or where to go. For the first time in my life, with everything going on, I just wanted to take the boys and go back to my parents' home. I can't be pregnant, I just can't; I kept telling myself.

That night after Chuck got home, we had a heart-to-heart talk. I told him I was done. I can't keep living like this. Always trying to please somebody else. I felt like the world was crashing in on me, smothering my life out of me. I didn't tell him I was leaving this time. I told him, "I want a divorce. I'm taking the boys and moving back home". It was at that moment those words frightened ME! Before we were married, Chuck and I talked about everything as we talked about getting married. If we had children, we would never fight in front of them. We would never go to bed mad at each other. We did have some long nights in those early years of married life (LOL). We'd always kiss each other good morning and goodnight. Every day we would make sure we said to each other, "I love you." And this one now frightened me; IF I ever ran back home to Mommy, he'd never let me come back. My Dad had told me when he gave me the are you sure you're ready to get married lecture, "If you ever run back home, I'm going to take you right back." There I was – stuck! If I left to go to my parents, my Dad was bringing me back, and Chuck wouldn't let me come back. And somewhere in that conversation, between these mind-boggling thoughts, I spouted out the words, "AND I'M PREGNANT!"

Chuck pleaded with me not to go; not to take his boys from him. "WE can do this together. We're going to have a baby, and maybe this is the girl you wanted. Things will get better when we come back from this trip."

. . . .

"Woe to you when all men speak well of you..." (Luke 6:26)

At the Assembly, the former State Youth Director, who we were scheduled to replace, came to Chuck and told him the position he was supposed to go to was no longer available, and he didn't have anywhere to go. He then asked if it'd be okay if he returned to Oregon as State Youth Director. "Of course," Chuck said, being the kind man he was. When he told me, I was beyond upset. "Now, what are we going to do? Did you forget your wife is PREGNANT? Do you remember we don't have a church, or a job, or a place to live?" Those words exploded out of my mouth. But like only Charles could do (I only called him that when times were tough, and I'm mad -smiles), he snuggled me up his arms and said, "Don't you think God knew this long before we did? We've trusted Him this far; we can't stop trusting Him now." All I could think to say was, "Can you get me some watermelon? I want watermelon NOW!" Watermelon will make this better, I'm sure.

I somehow managed to finish packing up our suitcases, while Chuck was out on the wild goose chase in downtown Dallas, Texas, looking to find me some watermelon. Oh yeah, and he did. He came in carrying a huge WHOLE watermelon. "I got you the biggest one I could find," he said, grinning from ear to ear. I was thankful he carried a pocketknife everywhere he went. We ate watermelon and more watermelon, and then a little more watermelon, before we started to leave. I often wondered what that housekeeper thought when she came to clean that room with all those watermelon rinds.

Chuck checked out at the front desk and then came back to the room just as the hotel room telephone rang. He answered and I heard him say, "We're leaving our hotel now, and I'll meet you at yours in fifteen minutes." It was a former pastor of Chuck's when he was a teenager, who'd become a second father to Chuck and his family. When I first met him, his rough voice scared me. But I'd come to love him and his family. He had just been appointed as the State Overseer of Idaho, and he had a church he wanted us to go pastor. He told us the parsonage was in the basement of the church, but, "You'll never know you're in the basement because it has daylight windows." Now isn't that just like God. Here we were, practically homeless, definitely jobless, and about to become a family of five...and God shows up when you think He's nowhere around.

Lewiston, Idaho was our new home. Definitely in a base-ment! We had to find a stick outside to knock off all the cobwebs that covered the entrance. We walked in and the "You won't know you're in a basement because it has daylight windows" comment...there were little 24-inch-high windows at the ceiling of the living room. It was dirty. The bathroom was upstairs, where the sanctuary was. Just a little note: you didn't delay your shower to just before a church service time' or you could be caught running down the stairs in your bath-robe. (LOL) There was a drain in the center of the kitchen in case the water overflowed. I sat down on the sofa, the only piece of furniture in the living room, and all four legs shot out like a cannon; the sofa was now on the floor. And you guessed it, I cried. I bawled. I wished. . . now if only my head would stop hurting. Chuck assured me we could make this a home, at least until the baby came, and then we'll do something different. And we did. We bought used furniture; beds, dressers, and a cradle for the soon-coming baby. "She" (our thoughts and the doctor's words per "her" heartbeat) was due on March 5th, my Dad's birthday.

The months ahead were never dull. I would let the boys go outside to play and tell them as long as I can see your legs running by the windows, you can play outside. The two of them would come up to the window, squat down and wave at me. Those memories I will always cherish. I did a lot of lying on the sofa. I craved watermelon and peanut butter and jelly sandwiches. I would go to the doctor and he would lecture me on my weight gain. I would stop by Dairy Queen on the way home and order me a milkshake and say, "Here's to you, Doc!" WHAT was I thinking? It felt good at the moment, but I was the one going to pay for it.

March was just around the corner. I saw the doctor, and he told me, you are nowhere near delivery. I would order another milkshake to combat the depression. Time dragged. The headaches never stopped. I never had any morning sickness throughout the whole pregnancy, but the headaches were almost unbearable. I saw the doctor on April 2nd, almost a month late now from the original due date of March 5th. I was in tears when I left after he told me at least another two weeks. I didn't even stop for the milkshake.

Chuck was working the graveyard shift. He came home the next morning at 8:00am. No sooner had he laid down in bed, I had my first pain. Again, that awful pain in my back. Never in any of my pregnancies did the "labor" start in my stomach, nor did my water ever break, as the doctor's told me were signs I was "in labor." Each one started in my back. But I knew, in spite of what the doctor had told me twenty-four hours earlier, this was for real. After an hour, I woke Chuck up and said I think I should go to the hospital.

He got up and called the doctor. They told him, she's not in labor, we just saw her yesterday, and she's two weeks away. Then with Chuck explaining my pain to them over the phone, they finally said, "Okay, why don't you bring her to the doctor's office." We got dressed and headed to the doctor's office. It was now 10:30am. I could not walk the long way on the sidewalk because of the pain, so we cut across the lawn area heading for the door. I was having "pushing" pains and trying not to push. They took me to a room quickly. The doctor finally came in, took one look at me, and said, "Oh God, get her to the hospital and fast!"

Thankfully, the hospital was across the street. When we entered by the registration desk, it was 10:45am. The doctor was right behind me, yelling, "Get her to delivery; forget the prep." Chuck stayed behind, signing me in.

The pain was only getting worse. I told the nurse, "I have to go to the bathroom; NOW!" She looked at me, smiled and said, "Honey, you're not going to the bathroom; you'll have this baby in there. You're going to delivery." I vaguely remember being transferred from the wheelchair to the gurney, but I remember those silver doors swinging open wide as everyone was running and rushing with me on that gurney.

It was 11:10am, and the crying of my baby was the most beautiful sound. The doctor looked up at me and said, "You've got a boy." "A boy?" I questioned, "You told me I was having a girl." The doctor had told me throughout the pregnancy that it was a girl. My mom had told me, "Linda, it's a boy. I can tell by the way you're carrying it." My mom did not miss many calls like that, and no, she wasn't a nurse. But I didn't listen. In fact, everything I had for the baby was PINK! The baby shower had produced nothing but pink. This baby boy was not going to like being dressed in pink.

I heard the doctor when he stepped outside the delivery room and said, "Mr. Querry, you have a son." Then I heard Chuck say, "I'm happy as long as he is healthy." Charles Querry, I thought, YOU promised me a girl!

Now, we needed a name, and Stephanie Lavone would not work anymore. A nurse suggested when she heard this, as I was looking into his eyes, that I name him Steven Lavon. I looked at this beautiful little boy in my arms and said, "Nope, he's not a Steven." It took us a couple days, but Chuck walked in the last day I was in the hospital, as we were facing the possibility of putting "Baby Querry" on the Birth Certificate, and said, "I think he looks like a Rodney. A Rodney Wade." I looked at him again, yep, he's definitely a Rodney Wade! Not only did we hold this baby, but this baby held us together.

Being a mom to three boys has been the greatest joy for me and their Pop. I wouldn't trade those years raising them for anything. We talked about adopting a little girl...until one day, Rodney started school. I never talked about adoption after that. We were blessed by God with the three boys we had, and they grew up to be three great young men. Did they ever make mistakes? Oh yeah! But the one thing we tried to let them know was no matter how bad or how big the mistake was, we were there for them to get them through it. Each one of them as adults have had times where they've failed, faced a defeat, or struggled to survive after a loss in their jobs, in their family, or in themselves personally. But the one thing they each have done is get back up, dust themselves off, and push through whatever pushed them down.

Since losing my husband, they've been my strength when I had none. When I've said numerous times, "I can't do this!" they've continuously told me, "Mom. You're stronger than you think. You CAN do it."

Today, when someone asks me, "How are you doing?" my words are always, "I'm okay." I've told some of my family and closest friends, "I'm okay from the outside, but on the inside I'm a broken woman." But this broken woman is becoming stronger every day. That doesn't mean I won't still cry. That doesn't mean memories won't trigger that huge lump that shows up in my throat and pushes water from my eyes. That part of me probably will never change. One of the things my husband would say to me when I was facing something I didn't think I could do, he'd tell me, "Toughen up, Tiger, you've got this!" His words still ring in my head when I think I'm going under.

But the most important thing I've learned walking this journey of grief these past five years is that I serve a God who goes before me. Nothing happens that He isn't aware of. Nothing takes place on this pathway I'm on that God hasn't already made a way where I might think there was no way.

No matter how many times I break down
There is always a little piece of me that says
No, you're not done yet, Get BACK UP!
- Author unknown

Chapter 16

the many costumes of fear

A passenger in a taxi leaned over to ask the driver a question and gently tapped him on the shoulder to get his attention. The driver screamed, lost control of the cab, nearly hit a bus, drove up over the curb, and stopped just inches from a large plate window.

For a few moments, everything was silent in the cab. Then, the shaking driver said, "Are you OK? I'm so sorry, but you scared the daylights out of me..." The badly shaken passenger apologized to the driver and said "I didn't realize that a mere tap on the shoulder would startle someone so badly."

The driver replied, "No, no, I'm the one who is sorry, it's entirely my fault. Today is my very first day driving a cab. I've been driving a hearse for 25 years..."

Fear comes dressed in so many costumes. The dictionary defines it as "an unpleasant, often strong emotion caused by anticipation or awareness of danger, an anxious concern...." According to the Smithsonian Magazine (October 27, 2017), it tells us that *"Fear starts in the part of the brain called the amygdala. A threat stimulus, such as the sight of a predator, triggers a fear response in the amygdala, which activates areas involved in preparations for motor functions involved in fight or flight!"*[10]

Fear may be something that at the moment scares us spitless, but later we find ourselves laughing hysterically about it.

That reminds me of what our family calls the flight of the "Cheerios." My youngest son, Rodney, was home for a visit, sitting in my husband's recliner one night after "everyone" had gone to bed. He was enjoying a rather large bowl full of Cheerios, watching television in the dark. My husband came up behind him (innocently) in the chair and said, "Goodnight, son," and the bowl full of Cheerios took flight. Cheerios were everywhere! Milk ran down my very frightened son's face, as my husband was now on the floor laughing hysterically picking up Cheerios. I was still finding Cheerios in places in that living room months later. To this day, when this story is mentioned, we all bust out in uncontrollable laughter. But it was total FEAR that night for Rodney.

Then there were the times I would play "rapture" games on my husband. I would see him drive in from work. I'd turn on the water in the kitchen sink, leave my shoes just as if I'd been standing there, run and gather up all three of our boys and we would go and hide quietly in a closet. My husband would come in, see the water running, my shoes there, and start calling out our names.... "Kevinnnn, Rannnndy, Rodneeey, then a strong LINNNDA! .... where are youuuu?

---

10 "What Happens in the Brain When We Feel Fear." Smithsonian Magazine, 27 Oct. 2017. https://www.smithsonianmag.com/science-nature/what-happens-brain-feel-fear-180966992/

I KNNNOW you're here, and the rapture didn't take place, I'm STILL here."

Now I'm sure you're saying, "Shame on you, Linda, that's just wrong!" Wrong? No. That was paybacks. Payback for the times I would come home from work, his car in the driveway, but I couldn't find him in the house. Thinking he was probably in the garage or outside, I'd go into the bedroom to change clothes. Open the sliding closet door, and he'd jump out at me screaming, "GOTCHA!" Or maybe the times I'd walk into a room, and he'd be hiding behind the door and jump out at me. Then there were those times I'd be doing dishes, my mind a hundred miles away, and he'd sneak up behind me and tap me on the shoulder. My sweet husband had an ornery streak that never quit. I cannot even tell you how many times now I wish he'd jump out at me and yell, "Gotcha!"

Those types of fear are momentary. You find yourself laughing at them after they are over.

Then there is "grief" fear! The fear that makes you weak in the knees when you walk back into your house that used to be your "Home," ALONE - the first time. When you need advice about a decision you have to make and he is not there to talk you through making the right decision. When the "change oil" light comes on in the car. When the tires need replacing. When the car breaks down. When the smoke alarm is constantly beeping, and it is too high for you to reach to change the battery. When a decision is at the dead-line, and you don't know what to do. When you have to move and don't know where to go or if you should go. When you want to go eat at your favorite restaurant, but you are not sure you can sit alone because he is not there. When someone asks you out, and you haven't dated in twenty – thirty

- forty - fifty years. Your "courage tank" springs a leak or is completely drained, and you are frozen in your steps.

When fear smacks you in the face and you are afraid you will forget! Forget every little detail about what your life was, knowing "what was, will never be again!" Fear that your memories are beginning to fade. Fear you will forget what his voice sounded like. Fear when you feel like the world keeps moving onward and it's pushing you right along with it, as if you are in a crowd of people rushing to get somewhere fast, when you just want to scream "STOP!" "STOP pushing me! STOP spinning!"

The lists are endless. You have questions, without answers and no one to talk it over with. Those fears push you against a wall and paralyze you. You remember in times past when your soulmate was there making those tough decisions, fixing those issues, and you depended on them more than you realized – until now. Now it's just you.

I remember a couple years ago hearing just a brief part of a sermon by Steven Furtick, Founder and Senior Pastor of Elevation Church in Charlotte, North Carolina. He was preaching at a time in my life when I felt like I was so alone. He said,

> **"**You're going through some stuff right now.
> Seems like God's abandoned you.
> Seems like God forgot about you.
> He didn't!
> Seems like God has left you all alone.
> He didn't!
> Seems like you're out there on your own.
> You're not!
> Seems like God is not working.

He is!

And He'll take the very thing the devil wanted to destroy – what's in you, the foundation of your life - and bring you into the place He's promised. **" "**

Can you identify with that?

• • • • • • • • • • • • • • •

One of the most fearful moments in my life was leaving a large, beautiful church. We had accepted the church, which was out of California, eighteen months earlier. It was our first experience of the "empty-nest syndrome," leaving all three of our now-grown sons at the same time. It had been a tough decision in the first place to make and to accept this pastorate, but we felt God was directing it. Trying to survive the absence of our boys at home was tough, and pastoring a tough church did not make it any easier. Unless you're a pastor and have experienced that, you probably will not understand these words...it was hellish! We were challenged with everything we did. Criticism from Council Members seemed endless.

I taught the most amazing group of young adults who wanted a change, but a change did not look promising during our pastorate. Council meetings would last way past midnight, arguing over trivial things. Harsh and angry words said to us were hurtful. Our mailbox was knocked down with a baseball bat by one of the Council Member's son's more than once. All because they had never accepted the resignation of their former pastor, who had been there for thirty-plus years. Before we came, the church had split under the first "buffer" pastor, and we had tried to reconnect it back. After contacting several Overseers of our church organization, we finally made the decision to leave – even though we had no place to go.

The night before we were leaving, we had 35 of my young adult class in our living room, begging us to stay. They told us we could all go and start our own church and leave this group of people, and "If you leave, we're leaving too." I listened as Chuck told them, "No, we're not going to stay. It's time for us to go. And you all shouldn't leave. The church needs you, and we are praying the next pastor will be the pastor that will make the difference."

Our U-Haul was loaded. As Chuck was putting the key in the door the next morning to lock up, the parsonage phone started ringing. There were only landlines and no cell phones, and normally there would be an "answering machine" (there I just dated myself-smiles) that would pick up with a recorded message, and you could leave a message. We had unhooked our answering machine to take with us. The phone kept ringing. I could tell by the look on his face that Chuck was about to go back in the house and answer the phone. I put my hand over his at the doorknob and said, "Let it ring. It's probably just another disgruntled Council Member." He locked the door, and we started down the steps toward the truck. The phone was still ringing. Chuck paused about halfway, turned around, and started back up the steps to the house and said, "I just feel like I should go answer it." I waited impatiently outside. I was scared that we had no place to go, but I was done with this place! About ten minutes passed before Chuck came out. As he locked the door, he said, "You are not going to believe this." He proceeded to tell me it was the Overseer from California.

This Overseer was not too happy when we had told him we had accepted a church out of state. But this morning, he told Chuck he was down on his knees praying, and all he could see was the face of Charles Querry, and the Lord spoke to him in his spirit and told him to get up right now and call him. He offered Chuck a church back in California – a church going through a horrific situation. Chuck said he felt immediately that this was a God-ordained appointment, and he accepted it.

We had no idea where we were going – but God did. That Overseer had no idea we were leaving our church – but God did. We had no idea where we would lay our head that night after we locked that door the first time – but God knew. And God knows where you are at right now. He has gone ahead of you, preparing the way before you ever get there.

Fear is a tactic the enemy puts on all of us. Fear can be a cage that the devil uses to paralyze and capture you and prevent you from being maximized to be the person you can be.

" You have a unique fingerprint that no one else has, to leave a unique imprint that no one else can leave. **"** [11]
**- Lead Pastor, Keith A. Craft,
Elevate Life Church, Frisco, Texas**

Isaiah 43:1 [NKJV] tells us, *"Do not fear, for I have redeemed you; I have called you by your name; you are mine."*

God knows your name. He calls you by name! He knows your fears. He knows where you are at right now.

Throughout our ministry those 52 years, it was times like these that taught me to trust God – not understand

---
11 "Your Divine Fingerprint", p.10

Him – but "trust" Him! To know that when "fear" tried to engulf me, that fear just wanted to send me to my room and shut out the world around me. But it has been those times of testing that I learned there are no surprises to God. Remember what I wrote earlier, God is not surprised. He did not wake up this morning and start pacing heaven's floors saying, "Oh, goodness, I did not see this coming!" (Remember, the scripture tells us, "He doesn't slumber or sleep!")

In the many, many times these past five years that the enemy has tried to fill me with fear, it has been seeing God at work ahead of me, that's gotten me through the loss of my husband. Oh, yes, there's been plenty of times I've screamed at God. WHY GOD? WHY US? WHY ME? WHY MY HUSBAND? Then I'd crash to the floor in a puddle of tears, because there was no answer from God, as I was pounding the carpet wet from my tears. Then in that moment of desperation, I would feel a calmness come over me, and a strength would rise up inside of me, allowing me to pull myself up off the floor and go a little farther.

There have been many of those "raising the Titanic" churches, but Chuck never stopped until a church became a better church. He built churches up and literally built church buildings. He bought better parsonages. He remodeled churches to make them better, and the many parsonages he made better are uncounted in my brain today.

But my husband's main goal never deviated from enlarging the Kingdom of God. He refused to be dominated by "fear," and I know he fought that in decisions he had to make. I have seen him so many times pick up a stranger on the highway so he could share Jesus with him. I have seen him see a homeless person on the street and pull over and take him somewhere, buy him a meal, and share Jesus with him. He has stood beside prisoners up for parole and told a judge to release them to him, and he will be responsible for their rehab. I have seen him wrestle people to the floor in a dingy, dirty apartment who were strung out on drugs, praying over them until they would settle down and agree to go to rehab. I have lost count of the many drunks who have staggered into our churches, smelly and reeking from alcohol, and he would wrap them up in his arms at an altar they had staggered to and pray with them until they would be sober and accept salvation. Then the numerous teenagers who felt they had a call on their life for ministry, and he would give them the opportunity to preach their first sermon. Those kids, now grown, are pastoring churches of their own or have become missionaries or teachers in Sunday School. He has taught for years in the Ministerial Training Program to prepare others for their ministry, and then seeing them go forward with their callings. He never allowed "fear" to dominate his life.

Remember that young eighteen-year-old girl that felt like jumping on the bed with the excitement of being a Pastor's wife? I am often reminded of that day so many years ago. I am also reminded that life in ministry has not always been a "bed of roses." There are tough times. There are fearful times. There are times, even, when you have the amazing love of parishioner's, you spend holidays alone. Your "best" friends are few and far between; and sometimes they desert you, hurt you, walk or move away from you. Your children are expected to be "perfect" because after all, isn't that what you're expected to be?

I had always tried, with everything in me, to be a nice person. I even tried hard not to kick the cow when she would kick over a pail full of milk. But I found out, rather quickly, that no matter how hard you tried to be sweet, nice, and friendly, there would be, at times, someone who would come against you for some forlorn reason.

However, after fifty-six years in pastoral ministry, I would do it all over again and then again. The great times outweigh the bad times every time. The people who have sat at your feet learning, the shy ones you have encouraged to be more than they thought they could be, the bold ones you have steered to be used by God with all their energy, the ones you have held in your arms through the loss of a loved one, the times you have joined lovers together in marriage, the children you have dedicated to the Lord, the long hours of planning and then seeing that vision come to fruition. The times you have been honored to "raise a sinking titanic" (i.e., church) and see its growth in enlarging the Kingdom of God. The children from Sunday School classes-now grown and using their talents for God. The troubled teens, who you have had a part in getting on the right path. The marriages you have saved through counseling. Helping seniors, who have felt abandoned with nothing to do, find they can stand at a doorway of the church with a smile greeting people.

Those lists are endless. Did I, did we, ever feel like quitting? Absolutely, there were times! We took sabbaticals for months. We retired three times. Each time saying, "That's it! We're done!" But each time, something burned deep inside us that spoke to us, "You are not finished yet!" You see, it's not to those who run the fastest, build the bests, or conquerors the most; it's to those who finish.

Our sons told their Pop so many times, "Pop, we don't want you to die behind a pulpit as a Pastor. We want you to retire and enjoy your life." After the last time Chuck was in church, we traveled back to southern California to be with our sons and for more tests. As we were crossing the "Grapevine" pass, Chuck reached over and took my hand as I was driving and said, "Sweetheart, except for a miracle from God, I won't preach again." He didn't. He left this world for heaven eighteen days later. But the thing I'll never forget was his response to the words his boys always told him about retiring. He would say, "If I die as a Pastor, it'll be the best day of my life." And that's exactly what he did.

You never know where your tiny little footsteps as a toddler will take you. But today, I am forever grateful for the footsteps that God chose for us, the paths we have crossed with many of you reading this book that we will cherish forever, and for the ones we have had an influence in helping their lives to become better. Remember this, and at the end of your journey, I hope you, like Charles Querry, can say, *"I have fought the good fight, I have run the race, I have kept the faith. Henceforth there is laid up for me the crown of righteousness, which the Lord, the righteous judge, will award to me on that Day..."* (1 Timothy 4:7,8 ESV)

One of my husband's last sermons was about Joseph's story (Genesis, Chapters 37-50). Joseph was raised in the most dysfunctional family ever...around tricksters, jealousy, and connivers...and he stayed true, stayed faithful, never complaining. Yet as "fearful" as some of the places Joseph's footsteps took him, God was true and faithful to him.

Don't let fear hold you hostage. Don't let your past dominate your future! Don't let the "stuff" going on around you take your focus off where you're headed! Don't let the "pit" become your home. Don't let this "prison" [of grief] be your stopping grounds. Be the person, like Joseph, that can change a nation.

I read this recently,

"Grief is like Glitter"

❝ You can throw a handful of it in the air; but when you try to clean it up, you will never get it all. Even long after the event, you will find glitter tucked in the corners. It will always be there...somewhere. ❞ [12]

The fearful times of grief will always be there – lurking in the corners of your mind – trying desperately to push you into a bedroom and lock the door. Get into bed, pull the covers over your head, and give up.

Someone once wrote this:

Start with Yourself!

When I was young and free, and my imagination had no limits, I dreamed of changing the world. As I grew older and wiser, I discovered the world would not change, so I shortened my sights somewhat and decided to change only my country.
But it too, seemed immovable.
As I grew into my twilight years, in one last desperate attempt, I settled for changing only my family, those closest to me, but alas, they would have none of it.
And now as I lie on my deathbed, I suddenly realize; if I had only changed my self-first, then by example I would have changed my family.

---

12 by Kevin Pádraig

From their inspiration and encouragement, I would then have been able to better my country and, who knows, I may have changed the world.[13]

As hard as it is to not allow fear to dominate our lives, and even though we may never change this world, we can know that we are still here for a reason, for a purpose. Finding that reason, that purpose, may just be the hardest part of your journey. But take that first step. You can do it!

---

13 Author unknown – These words are said to be written on the tomb of an Anglican Bishop in the crypts of Westminster Abbey in London, England

Chapter 17

from grief to grace

January – February - March 2017

"H appy" New Year? Well, it started off remarkably. Family Pictures. Disneyland with all the family-first time ever. My brother-in-law's 90th birthday celebration . . . and then everything changed . . .

January 19th, our whole family gathered in a park for family pictures, followed by an amazing trip to Disneyland.

January 23rd, Chuck and I flew to Oregon to celebrate his brother's 90th birthday. Such a strong giant of a man.

February 28th, Chuck's brother, that strong giant of a man, went to his eternal home in heaven.

March 1st, Chuck woke up with a horrible backache... and our nightmare began. The pain radiating down his leg only grew worse. We were planning another trip to Oregon, the first part of April, to his brother's Memorial service, which Chuck was part of officiating. Something had to change for him, and change fast. As the pain worsened and became unbearable, we made the first (of many) trips to the Emergency Room at the hospital. After waiting over ten hours in the Emergency Room waiting room, and I had made numerous trips to the reception window asking – no pleading – for someone to please see Chuck, as he was in horrible pain, we were finally called back. The doctor who saw him recognized he WAS in pain and came back with "her" diagnosis, "because of your age, you have arthritis in your hip. Go home and take some Tylenol." I was livid! I told her, "This is more than 'arthritis.' Can you please do an MRI?" Her response was, with a shrug of her shoulder and sarcasm in her voice, "An MRI isn't necessary! Just give him Tylenol," and she was gone.

Chuck was done! He just asked me, "Babe, please take me home so I can just lay down." I did. The Tylenol was useless. I gave him multiple doses of "over the counter" Ibuprofen, but nothing relieved the pain.

Chuck had just finished building a sound room in our church and had started a remodeling project on a parsonage beside the church. He had put in new cabinets, so it was "safe" to assume he had hurt his back doing that. I have had numerous back surgeries, and I know what sciatic pain down your leg feels like. All of his pain, along with his description, made me believe he had done something to his back.

After another failed diagnosis at the Emergency Room, with the aid of crutches, we prepared to make the trip to Oregon for his brother's service on April 8th. The flight required a wheelchair to transport him from the check-in to the gate and the gate to the sidewalk upon arrival. With the aid of lots of over-the-counter medication, and despite the pain, Chuck officiated the service. Chuck was a strong, strong man. He did not accept "no," "I can't," or "that's impossible" for answers. Our faith in God, lots of prayers, and back massages for him through those days helped, but nothing was relieving his pain.

April 12th was our 54th Wedding Anniversary. One thing we had always done, even when we were so poor (the poor people called us poor), was celebrate our anniversary, just the two of us. There were years when that meant just getting in the car and taking a drive in the country or by the beach. But it always ended up somewhere where Chuck would order that ONE Black Raspberry Milkshake with TWO straws, just like we had on our first date. It was years after we were married that he told me the story behind that ONE Black Raspberry Milkshake with TWO straws. That night of our first date, he only had twenty-five cents in his pocket. That was the cost of that milkshake. (Yeah, in 1962, things were different).

We had finally managed to get an appointment with our Primary doctor, praying she would help him. As we were driving to the appointment that day in Southern California, I reached over and took Chuck's hand and said, "I love you, Babe, and Happy Anniversary." He responded back with the same words and then said, "Sweetness, you know how we always do something special on our Anniversary?" I smiled and said, "Yes, but it's okay." He continued, "Well I've always tried to take you somewhere different every year. So, this year, I'm taking you to the doctor's office." We both laughed. That was just who he was. He would find something positive in every situation – and he would always make sure he made me laugh at some point every day. That anniversary will be an anniversary, along with the other fifty-three that I will cherish forever.

Our primary doctor never hesitated a moment when she saw the pain Chuck was in. In fact, she left the room and went and called an Orthopedic Doctor, and made an appointment for the next day with him. We saw the Orthopedic Doctor, who scheduled Chuck for an MRI the following day. When the results were in, the Orthopedic Doctor gave us the results. Chuck had two tumors on his spine at the L4 and L5, hence the reason for the sciatic pain. He also had a fractured hip. Wow! Something that a simple X-ray at one of the visits to the Emergency Room would have produced – right? The Orthopedic Doctor explained to us, he could fix the hip, but he could not remove tumors, so he referred us to a Neurosurgeon. Then he wanted Chuck to be in a wheelchair until he could do surgery on his hip so that the fracture did not become a break.

It was now the end of April. When we saw the Neurosurgeon, she wanted several more MRIs from his head to his toes. I explained to her, "he's in a lot of pain, and laying on that hard table doing an MRI is extremely painful." Even though our Primary Doctor had given him prescription pain meds, he was still in a lot of pain. Again, the Neurosurgeon explained she wanted to know "everything that was going on."

The MRIs were completed, and the Neurosurgeon scheduled us to see an Oncologist. Now you know when you hear that word, it is not good news.

May 15th, we met with the Oncologist, a little over a month since that first visit with our Primary. She walked into the room where Chuck, me, and two of our sons were waiting. She sat down, holding the folder in her hands between her legs, and spouted out, "Well, you know you have Stage

4 cancer."...cancer...cancer....cancer....as it echoed through that room.

WAIT! WHAT?

We were stunned – as if someone had just shot us with a stun gun! There were no words spoken as she rambled on, "...it's on your brain, your lungs, your adrenal glands, your hips, I need some biosp....." SHUT UP! I wanted to shout SHUT UP! SHUT YOUR MOUTH! Can you not see that this is the FIRST TIME we've heard this? Did you flunk the "bedside manners" class in Med school too????? WHO in their right mind, if they care anything about people, starts a sensitive conversation like that in that way? I wanted to take her license hanging on the wall and smash it at her feet, just like she'd just smashed our lives before us. Maybe a "throat-punch" would be appropriate here?

I vaguely remember the rest of her useless words that afternoon as she continued on with not one ounce of compassion in her voice... "you have six months to live..." WHAT? SIX months? Who died and made you a god? She continued, "Do you drink beer?" No, my husband responded. "Do you drink wine?" No, again, he replied. "Well, then, what do you do for fun?" "I'm a Pastor," Chuck said with a bit of irritation in his tone, "and that is what I enjoy!" I wanted to stand up and say, "And lady, you need Jesus too. Maybe that would help your attitude!" Chuck must have known I was more than a tad bit irritated as he reached over and took my hand in his, patting it with his other hand. He was not going to let me stand up and yell at her now. She continued, "Do you like ice cream?" "Yes," Chuck calmly replied, trying to diffuse the anger that now infiltrated that room. "Then eat a gallon every day because whatever you eat, the cancer will eat half of it," she replied. There that word was again ....cancer ...cancer ...cancer...echoing in my head like an explosion from a volcano with red hot lava oozing down my body. She rambled on about scheduling biopsies, which I'd never remembered had the nice girl at the front office not handed me a paper with them all written down. Why would a sweet girl like that work for a doctor like that? I thought as I shuffled away.

As we walked to the elevator, all of us still pretty much speechless, fighting back tears, Chuck reached for my hand, "Baby, don't worry, it'll be okay. We beat this once, and we'll beat it again!" Seven years earlier, he had been diagnosed with prostate cancer, and after radiation treatments, the cancer was completely destroyed. In fact, after all the tests done at this time, none of the cancer he was dealing with now had any connection with the prostate cancer.

Radiation to his brain was scheduled. The most loving Radiologist and Technicians ever! I'm sure they all got an A+ in their bedside manners class! Evidently, it was a different Med School than the Oncologist attended .... OKAY! I'll stop! "There are some lesions on his brain in various places," the Radiologist explained, "Something similar to a peppermint striped candy circular shape. We are scheduling twelve radiation sessions, and I feel confident we will get rid of all of them." Wow, good news for a change. I took a deep breath, maybe the first one in days.

We went to the hospital for the biopsies. Chuck was sedated, and they took him back for the first one. Within a few minutes, the doctor came out and told me the cyst in his lung was located directly behind the juggler vein and was very small. I cannot do it because if I puncture that vein, he will go straight to heaven. Then he went on to say, "I'm going to get approval from the insurance, and we will do the biopsy on the adrenal glands." Again, they took Chuck back. Again within a few minutes, the doctor came back and said, "The cyst on both adrenal glands is so small we cannot get a biopsy on either of them. Again, another deep breath. Things were looking so much better. They did the biopsy on the tumors on his spine, and we were told it was one of the most aggressive and fast-moving cancers.

But God!!!! Right?

The brain radiation was underway. We were hopeful. But the cancer was obviously filling up on half of everything Chuck was eating. He was losing weight fast.

We celebrated Memorial Day with our son and his family and a lot of other people at a park. Such a fun day. Later that week, we drove back to our home in Visalia, a three-and half-hour trip. June 4th was our last Sunday at church. We were planning to drive back to southern California for his radiation session later in the week. As I was driving us home from church that day, Chuck asked me to stop by and get Taco Bell for lunch. Taco Bell? He didn't like Taco Bell but would go there because he knew I loved it. I said, "Are you sure? You don't have to eat Taco Bell today just for me." He assured me that's what HE wanted, and he was hungry. So, I stopped and got it. As I pulled into the carport at home, I got his wheelchair out of the trunk. I helped him get in the wheelchair and turned to open the back door to get my purse when he had a seizure. He went totally stiff. Normally at our complex on any day, and especially Sundays, there are people standing around talking or watching their kids play everywhere. This day, no one was around anywhere.

I started screaming at the top of my lungs, trying to hold Chuck in the wheelchair. My phone was in my purse in the back seat. I prayed! I screamed! Nothing. I thought he had died. I somehow managed to push him up close enough to the car seat to wedge him in, and I reached over the seat and got my purse and phone. I dialed 911. I was still screaming "HELP!" when the operator answered the call.

I started explaining to her what was happening, when Chuck came to, sat up in the wheelchair, and asked me, "Who are you talking to Babe?" I asked him, "Do you know what just happened?" "What? I was getting in the wheelchair. Did you get us Taco Bell?" Have you ever lost a kid and was totally panicked, and then you found him and wanted to spank his bottom for running off, but you didn't because he was found? That is exactly how I felt that day. I didn't spank Chuck's bottom, but I did smother his face with kisses.

When we got into the house, I told him, lay down here on the sofa, I will get your Taco Bell. To which he said, "Ugh, I don't want anything. I'm just tired."

I quickly changed the clothes out from the suitcases and repacked with clean clothes. I was exhausted, but I didn't want to go through another episode like that again by myself. As I packed, Chuck rested, and then we headed back to our son's house in Southern California.

Randy had ordered everything he knew his dad would need. A hospital bed was set up and ready, and a small cot for me was beside it. It had been a long Sunday; we went to bed beside each other for the last time.

Monday night, we had just finished eating dinner and were sitting in the living room, watching a ballgame on TV. My daughter-in-law, Andi, had made Chuck's favorite food

- Spaghetti. I was carrying our plates back into the kitchen when Chuck started yelling out orders as if he were in the Navy (60 years ago), telling them if they didn't get that hole plugged, this ship is going down. I sat the plates down on the floor and went back to him. "Babe," I said, "look at me..." He looked at me and was yelling as if I was one of the sailors. "Sweetheart, stop, look at me, it's me, Linda..." Randy had already gone and called the paramedics; the ambulance was there. I went to find my shoes and came back as they were putting him in the ambulance. I jumped in the car with my son, and we followed. I could see Chuck in the ambulance, and for the first time in my life, I wondered if he was afraid. Why did I think I needed my shoes on? I should have been in there with him. I didn't want him to be alone with strangers – in an ambulance!

Arriving at the hospital, security was not going to let us through. My son, being a Police Officer, knew how to get where he needed to be. By the time we got to the room with Chuck, they were pumping him full of whatever that was hanging from that clear bottle above his bed. He began to recognize us and was asking what happened. The doctor told me they were admitting him for observation, and I could come to get him the next morning. When I got to the hospital the next morning, the doctor told me, "He's not going home. He's been in the Navy off and on all night. We need to keep him a few days and observe what's happening."

Chuck never came home again. That was June 5th. The doctors kept running ultra-scans, or tests that allowed him to stay five days. On day four, the doctor told me I needed to call in Hospice. HOSPICE? WHY? He's got six months!!!! I felt sick! I wanted to throw up! This isn't happening to me!

To us! This is a dream – no, a NIGHTMARE! I'm going to wake up, and it's all been nothing but a horrific nightmare. I felt like something had grown inside me, and was ripping me apart one organ at a time. NO ONE had prepared me for this!

Friday, June 10th, we had to move Chuck to a Nursing Facility due to insurance limitations for the hospital stay. When the doctor told me this, I said, "No, he's having surgery on his hip on Tuesday." "No, he's not Mrs. Querry. He's not having any surgery." "Yes, he is!" I argued, "It's already scheduled." The doctor took my hands in his and said, "Do you really want to put him through a hip surgery, with a long painful recovery, knowing he's only got days to live?" NO! NO! NO! My brain can't handle these death sentences. "He's got SIX MONTHS!" I managed to mutter as I felt my face slowly becoming wet from the moisture falling from my eyes. "She said he had six months!" I looked up at the face of the doctor now seated right in front of me, shaking his head back and forth as he said, "I'm so sorry, but no, he doesn't."

I wanted to yell, "LIAR, LIAR, HER PANTS ARE ON FIRE!" but there were no words coming out of my mouth. The doctor took me to another room, where two Hospice ladies were waiting for me. Thankful one of my sons was there too. I do not remember much of anything else after that, until what happened when Chuck saw heaven (read about it in Chapter 13), just before the ambulance came to transport him to the Nursing Facility.

Those next twelve days seemed just like a "resting point" because I truly believed God would heal Chuck, and we would walk out a living testimony. The way I prayed for Chuck's miracle and the way God gave him his miracle, was two completely different ways. I called this chapter "from grief to grace." The grief that rips your heart apart, and you think you'll die too when you get that phone call and they're gone, is hell on earth. I have suffered the most hellish experience of my life these past few years, grieving for my lover, my soul-mate, my best friend, my son's Pop, and my grandkid's Popa. I would not wish this on anyone. If you are reading this and you still have your spouse by your side, give them double, triple, and quadruple kisses and hugs and say, I love you, over and over and over again! Don't argue and fuss and fight. It's not worth it. Cherish your moments together because you have no guarantee when you won't have those moments anymore.

. . . .

I am thankful I got to live the "and they lived happily ever after" story. Oh, don't think there weren't some thorns on some rose bushes. But "we" made up our mind, as hurtful as the thorns might be, there would be more roses to bloom than thorns.

I'm "living" (maybe "existing" is a better word), the loss of my love. And I cannot even count the times I've begged him to come back. But WHY would he ever want to come back? His journey ended here on earth with one breath, one heartbeat, and the next one he started in his eternal home. It's God's "grace" to me, his "favor" on me, that is what has got me through this tough journey, and I've tried to do it gracefully. My husband's book, that God wrote about him, was finished on June 22, 2017, but mine wasn't. That first year without him, I was in such a fog I barely remember anything but tears, sobbing tears. Year two was the worst because that year shook me to the reality that he was gone and he was not coming back. Year three, I tried to focus on what I was doing, where I was going, and if I could even make it. The waves are farther between, yet they still come. A song comes on the radio that we used to sing together, and my eyes are tear-soaked again. But it is different this year. It's not like a car slammed on its brakes in front of me, and I slammed into his rear end. Shocked. Whiplashed. Unable to move. I am a little more aware of the triggers ahead of me and try to prepare myself a little better. His birthday. Our Anniversary. Christmas. Trick or Treating with my granddaughters on Halloween. I have begun to accept that all those things now are different. It's still his birthday. It's still our Anniversary. It's still Christmas, or Thanksgiving, or Halloween – it is just a different kind of holiday this year.

And as the years continue on, four – five? How in the world did I make it FIVE years, Babe, without you? I did it because of God's grace. God's favor on me because I strive to continue to walk this journey of grief and do it as gracefully as I possibly can.

You see, today I feel like this...but if you drop by tomorrow, you may have to pick me up off the floor from my puddle of tears because I still have to give myself time to grieve and maybe even heal someday – in the future – if that is even possible.

Chapter 18

learn to dance with a limp

read this as often as I need to to get me through a tough day, a tough week, or any time I feel like I just might be losing my mind.

The Widow and Widower's Cry

"Despite what you might think, the tears that come to me are necessary. My tears are because I loved someone with all my heart and I can't be with them, touch them, kiss them, or hug them again. Not even once.

Do you know how that feels?

I cry because I loved. I cry because I lost. I cry because I can still feel......everything. I cry because this is so unfair and there's nothing, I can do to change it.

These tears come in the shower, on my long run, in the car at the stoplight and parking lots, in public bathrooms, under my covers in bed, while cooking dinner and taking out the trash, when nothing goes right, in the darkness and in the daylight. They come for a reason and a season.

Sometimes I cry because of the past memories, sometimes because I'm moving forward courageously, sometimes because I'm confused and lost, sometimes because I'm exhausted and over it and sometimes when I'm profoundly, positively happy.

They are healing, inconvenient, embarrassing, breathtaking, uncontrollable, and unyielding and as mysteriously beautiful and scared as love is to me. In fact, without love, these tears would have no meaning whatsoever.

These brave tears wouldn't percolate at all if I had not found the courage to give my whole heart to another. To fully commit myself heart-to-heart, infinitely.

So, if you see me tear up or break down, find me a tissue, give me a hug, hold my hand, find a private place we can go and sit together until it passes. Hold that space with me. Your kindness genuinely helps this feel less awkward.

Thank you ahead of time. Having a golden friend like you in a moment like this is the silver lining of every tear I shed. Some of my tears will come alone in silence, but all of my tears come calling out for compassion, friendship and connection.

Let's be willing and grateful for this authentic way to emotionally connect with each other and better understand the deeper meaning in all our tears. Let it rain until it releases our pain as we regain the hope and strength to face another moment in this storm after loss.

Dedicated to every widow and widower who has cried from the core of their precious broken heart. **"** [14]

There, that's me! I have said that. I have thought that. I have lived that!

If there is anything that I absolutely cannot handle, it is when someone is standing in front of me, trying to "comfort" me, saying, "I know how you feel" while they are standing there holding hands with their spouse. Bull-sit! I said, "sit" (eye roll). Sit down and shut up! Until you have walked in the shoes of a widow or widower, you haven't got a clue!

I am not talking about a divorce, and I am sure, absolutely, that is a journey all its own. I am not talking about losing your mom or dad, and I have lost both, and that is not easy. Suddenly you feel like an orphan. I am not talking about losing a child. Dear Lord, I cannot even imagine that kind of pain. I have never experienced that, so I can only imagine. I am talking about this journey of grief when you lose your spouse, your lover, your best friend, the one who cuddled you in their arms on your tough days, the one who kissed away your fears, the one who gave you the security that everything will be okay someday. You cannot tell me how to live, how to grieve, or when to stop grieving. You cannot tell me that I need to "move on" or when to "get over it."

Do you know what it's like to hear a doctor give you a death sentence? Do you know what it's like to stand by their side and watch them, in a matter of a few weeks, drop down to skin and bones? Or walk in and find them gone – gone forever! Do you understand the "alone" feeling you feel in a room full of friends, or just people? Do you realize that not

---

14 Sturgis, Gary. "The Widow and Widower's Cry." Coping With Bing, 6 Nov. 2022, coping-withbing.com/the-widow-and-widowers-cry/.

only am I grieving my soulmate, my best friend, my lover, but I am also grieving who I was when they were here by my side? That "me" died with them. That "me" isn't the "ME" I was all those years. This "me" is different now. So, you cannot tell me when or even how I am supposed to be living. I am living with part of "me" gone, and that "me" will never be the same again!

One writer wrote this: *"I was tired of well-meaning folks, telling me it was time I got over being heartbroken. When somebody tells you that, a little bell ought to ding in your mind. Some people don't know grief from garlic grits. There are some things a body ain't meant to get over. No, I'm not suggesting you wallow in sorrow, or let it drag on; no, I am just saying it never really goes away. (A death in the family) is like having a pile of rocks dumped in your front yard. Every day you walk out and see them rocks. They're sharp and ugly and heavy. You just learn to live around them the best you can. Some people plant moss or ivy; some leave it be. Some folks take the rocks one by one and build a wall."*
\- Michael Lee West, American Pie

I recently found the website elephantjournal.com. Reading some of the statements, I came across this one by Anne Lamott. She writes:

❝ You will lose someone you can't live without, and your heart will be badly broken, and the bad news is that you never completely get over the loss of your beloved. But this is also good news. They live forever in your broken heart that doesn't seal back up. And you come through. It's like having a broken leg that never heals perfectly – that still hurts when weather gets cold, but you learn to dance with the limp.

"Grief doesn't come and go in an orderly, confined timeframe. Just when we think the pangs of anguish have stolen our last breath, another wave sweeps in and we are forced to revisit the memories, the pain, the fear. We fight against the currents, terrified of being overwhelmed...lost in our brokenness.

"Yet, grief, as painful a season as it is, is a necessary part of healing. **"**

So, what will you do with your pile of rocks? Will you stop dancing? Or will you take those rocks, one by one, and somehow, maybe a lot slower than anyone thinks you should, and build a beautiful wall, maybe you'll even paint a mural on that wall. But whatever you do, keep dancing – even if it's with a limp.

Chapter 19

tearing and mending

"**M**aybe if we still tore our clothes today, people would understand the grief we're experiencing. . .

"There's this Jewish practice of rendering one's clothes called the 'keriah.' When you lost a loved one, you entered into a formal time of grieving that involved the rendering or tearing of garments. It was a public and powerful expression of grief. Today's ritual is less spontaneous and more regulated: the garment is cut by a rabbi at a funeral service, as the bereaved recite words relating to God's sovereignty. One tradition says that the mourner must tear the clothing over the heart – a sign of a broken heart.

"And then there were special guidelines for how the mending was handled. Depending on the loss you sustained, you might be able to permanently repair your clothing. Other losses required that you never fully close the tear. We too, as a family are torn, in need of mending.

"Tearing and mending is the best way to describe death and loss and I'm learning we can't really put life back together again until we've faced the coming apart... **"** [15]

When I first read this article, I was reminded of my first time returning back to "our" home alone. Remember me slumped in "his" recliner, hugging the pillows that had supported his painful leg? I sobbed into those pillows that night, tearing at my shirt I had on until I ripped it. I didn't care. I felt like that was what was happening to my insides; they were being ripped out.

The Bible in the Old Testament speaks of "sackcloth and ashes" as a symbol of debasement, mourning, and/or repentance. Someone wanting to show his repentant heart would often wear sackcloth, sit in ashes, and put ashes on top of his head. Sackcloth was a coarse material usually made of black goat's hair, making it quite uncomfortable to wear. The ashes signified desolation and ruin.

When someone died, the act of putting on sackcloth showed heartfelt sorrow for the loss of that person. Very simply, sackcloth and ashes were used as an outward sign of one's inward condition. It showed a visible sign of one's grief. Now I am not suggesting all of us on this journey of grief change our garments to sackcloth and sit in a pile of ashes or walk around with ashes on our heads.

However, when you think about this, wouldn't it be easier at times if people could actually "see" where we were at on this journey? If we approached someone with our garments torn, or a garment of sackcloth with ashes on our head, do you think people would have an "a-ha moment" and have a

15 Excerpts from "The Sacred Work of Tearing & Mending: Life After Death, by Heather Riggleman

sudden insight like, "Whoa, they are still grieving, I need to be here for them. I need to be gentle."

Grief doesn't come and go in an orderly, confined time-frame. Just about the time we think the piercing spasm of pain has stolen our last breath, another wave sweeps in, and we are forced once again to revisit the memories. We fight against the currents, terrified of being overwhelmed and lost in our brokenness all over again. In some of my deepest depths of grieving, my thoughts would go to the place: "What if I don't stop crying this time? What if this is the end for me and I cannot recover." Those are the moments when the ripping of your clothes would be so easy to do.

People have told me, "Do not get stuck in grief." I'm pretty sure I've been there, and some days I fear I am there. They tell us you have to move quickly through this process. Whatever you do, do not tarry there very long. Yet, to run from grief is to run from the very thing that can bring calmness in the pain of our loss.

Grieving is the most difficult time, but it is also a time that must happen to allow ourselves to survive this horrific loss. This road has speed bumps and potholes. You are traveling "solo," and some days, you will move a little slower over the speed bumps. Other days you will fall hard into a pothole, and you have to struggle to get back up. Do not gauge your journey on how fast or slow you are going. Gauge it on making it "through."

An anonymous person wrote this: "I'll be okay – just not today." I'm still waiting for the tomorrow when I will be okay.

Chapter 20

dreams and/or visions

The sunlight in my bedroom window causes me to squint my eyes. I reach over to the other side of the bed to touch his hand – then reach a little farther; slowly, I turn my head to look, but he is not there. The covers on his side of the bed have not moved. No! No! It was real! He was here, holding me in his arms, telling me everything was going to be okay. But it was not okay, not now, not ever. I bury my head in his pillow, trying to soften the sobbing tears raging from my body. WHY did I open my eyes? WHY did I wake up? It is real! He's gone!!

I manage to get up. My legs feel like lead weights have been attached to them. I make my way to his recliner in the living room. It's dark. Maybe I will fall asleep. Then I see it, there in the corner ahead of me, a light flashing like an SOS warning. I look around. It's totally dark outside. If there is not a light on anywhere, then where is this flashing light coming from? My eyes are burning from the sobbing. Then, as if someone had entered the room, a calmness comes over me, and the sobbing stops. I cannot take my eyes off the flashing light. I have pulled his pillow from the bed up close to my chest now, watching, waiting for it to disappear. It doesn't. Finally, I speak softly, "Babe, is that you? Are you here?" the words slowly come from my lips. The light keeps flashing. "You ARE here, aren't you, sweetheart." My voice now gaining excitement, "You ARE here!!!!" I don't take my eyes off the flashing light. "Sweetheart, are you here? I have to know," now once again, I feel my voice slowly softening. The light flashes three fast times, and it's gone. I know it was him. I know he was here! I know those three flashes were "I love you." Words he told me every day from the day we met. I know that was him.

And now, as you are reading this, you're probably saying, "Yep, she HAS lost it. She has gone crazy. She needs help." But think and say what you want, there have been so many times that I know God has allowed him to show up in a dream or light or in some way to let me know, he is near.

A few days later, after coming back to "our" home, I knew I couldn't continue sleeping in his recliner. As I turned down the bed, instead of stacking ALL the pillows nicely on the floor as usual, I tossed them to the other side of the bed, letting them fall wherever they landed. I felt like I was in an "out of body" mode. Nothing seemed real. I climbed into bed and exhausted from lack of sleep, I fell asleep quickly, only to be awakened feeling kisses on my face. I opened my eyes just in time to see his shadow walking away down the hallway. "Come back, sweetheart!" I tried to scream, "Chuck, come back." But he was gone. In that moment, I felt he came to tell me goodbye one more time. I never saw his shadow again. But think what you may, after fifty-five years together, I would know his shadow anywhere. I was not dreaming. I was wide awake, awakened by his kisses on my face like he would wake me up so many mornings.

The first birthday of his, we celebrated together. My granddaughter, Aubrey, organized it all. After dinner at The Ole Spaghetti Factory (his favorite), we walked to the beach to release white balloons. Our family wrote messages of our own on our individual balloons and then released them, singing, "Happy birthday to you." One of the kids videoed it. When you watch that video, you see a white butterfly. That white butterfly stops by each one of our feet for just a moment and then flies on to the next, then the next. I know you think it's crazy, but I believe that was my husband letting us know he was there.

Shall I go on?

• • • • • • • • • • • • • •

On the morning my husband passed away, our nephew, Scott, and two of his friends from work decided to play hooky and go surfing at the ocean in Seaside, Oregon. Scott does not surf, and as he swam, a riptide hit him and drug him out. The waves were bashing him up against a big slick, and very tall rock. After a while, he decided to swim around to the other side of the rock, thinking maybe the waves would not be as bad. So, he did, but now his friends could not see him. Another riptide hit him, dragging him even farther out. He had tread water for an hour and a half. Finally, exhausted, he knew he couldn't keep it up. He said he was thinking, "I'm just going to lay on my back, and these waves will bash me into those rocks, and it will all be over." As he was trying to lay back, he heard a voice saying, "Keep treading!" He said again, "I can't!" Again, as he tried to lay back on his back, he heard a voice say, "Keep treading. Your mom cannot handle losing two people today." Within a few minutes, the Coast Guard Helicopter spotted him and picked him up. Scott believed that voice was his Uncle Chuck. At that time, he had no idea his Uncle Chuck had passed away early that morning at about the same time he was almost drowning in that ocean.

The day before Chuck passed away, he had been asleep. He woke up and immediately said, "He's safe, he's saved, they're all saved." We had no clue who or what he was talking about at the time. But now, pretty sure, it was Scott...and maybe as the angels were carrying Chuck to heaven that morning, they flew by the coast of Seaside, Oregon, and shouted "Keep treading" to my nephew Scott.

I know, unless you have experienced dreams or visions after losing your loved one, you are probably pretty convinced that I have lost it. But I assure you, I am in my right mind!

The dreams I have had have always come at a time when I needed some reassurance that he was still near me. The first surgery I went through after Chuck was gone, I was petrified. It was a major surgery to replace my neurostimulator and all the wires that ran down my back. The recovery period was long and painful. Chuck was always there to help me out of bed and in and out of a shower, especially the first three weeks. The night before the surgery, I had two dreams. They were so real. I saw him walking up to my hospital bed in a white "doctor-like" shirt, and he just stood there taking my hand. Because it seemed so real, I quickly opened my eyes because I knew I would see him. I didn't. He was gone, and now so was the dream. I fell back asleep and had a second dream. This time I was in the living room near the sofa, sitting in an office chair, reclining back. I leaned farther back, and the chair started flipping over backwards. I screamed and looked up just as the chair froze, and Chuck caught me, just smiling down at me. I remember waking up thinking, I am not alone. He just confirmed that he is here with me and he will always catch me.

Shortly after Chuck went to heaven, I would find myself looking into the heavens and asking, "What are you doing up there, Babe?" He never answered. One particular time, asking God the "why?" questions and getting no answers, I felt frustrated. I needed something. I needed answers. A few nights later, I had another dream. Chuck and I had matching emerald green suits we had purchased one year for Christmas pictures. It always amazed me the times, without even knowing what each other was wearing, we would show up together in those suits. He always got up early and left for church before I did. Many times, I didn't even see him on Sunday mornings until I got to church. I would walk in and we would both be in those emerald green suits. In this dream that night, Chuck came flying towards me, you guessed it, in his emerald green suit with his beautiful wings. He reached for my hands. . .I woke up, sitting up in bed with both hands reaching straight up. I didn't get to grasp his hands that morning, but such a calmness came over me after that, that I had not felt in days. Those unanswered questions seemed okay for that moment. He had his wings. He was flying! The hospital clothes were no longer part of his attire. He was pain-free. That was enough answers for me that day.

Alan Eiser, a psychologist and clinical lecturer at the University of Michigan Medical School in Ann Arbor, says, *"dreams can be 'highly meaningful,' because they 'deal with the sort of personal conflicts and emotional struggles that people are experiencing in their daily lives.'"* (December 30, 2021)

Emotional struggles? Yes! That has been a huge part of what grief has been and still is in my life. Yet, I cling to every dream, every momentary sight I might see that just might be him letting me know he is still watching over me.

We used to lay in bed on New Year's Eve, and we would "dream" together about the things we wanted to see and do in the upcoming new year. We both could have some wild imaginations. There were times when we would clasp each other's hands and shout, "Let's do it! Together we can do it!" Then we would burst out laughing as the clock struck midnight. As our kisses ended the year, we would drift off to sleep with those dreams on our minds. So many of those dreams came true, so many we were cheated out of when he was called to his eternal home. Too soon for me. Obviously, just right for God's plan. Now it's up to me, first, to find new dreams and, secondly, to see those dreams come true because that is what Chuck would want me to do.

Chapter 21

"Pop" the hero in our family
Written by my 3 sons

I am very proud of my three sons and the young men they are today. Are they perfect? No. Have they made mistakes and failed? Yes, haven't we all? But in each of those times of mistakes and failures, they've gotten back up, pulled themselves together, and continued trying to be the best person they can be. Each of them had a great relationship with their dad. One of the things we tried to instill in them as we were raising them was that there was nothing so bad or so awful that they could not come to us and tell us, and together we would work it out. That is exactly what they did. Even today, we still work together to make things better when they aren't. We say we are **#QUERRYSTRONG**! in this journey of grief and them missing their Pop, their dad, their "best friend" with whom they could talk about anything. They have fought through times of loneliness, depression, and, yes, even tears that at times still fall today. Following are three articles, one from each of them, as they tell who their Pop was to them.

Written by Kevin, our firstborn son, after the loss of his Pop, on June 22, 2017, and read at his father's Celebration of Life service July 22, 2017

. . . .

"Pop's Fingerprints"

On behalf of my mother, Linda, my brothers, Randy and Rod, and the entire Querry family, I would like to express our heartfelt thanks to each one of you that have joined us today from near and far to celebrate the Life, Legacy, Ministry, and Fingerprints of THE Reverend, Doctor, Bishop, Pastor, Babe, Pop, Poppa, Great Poppa, Uncle Charles "Chuck" Clifton Querry. You all are more than friends; you are our family. Your presence here today affirms that Pop's Fingerprints have made a great imprint upon your lives.

Only one life, it will soon be past, and only what's done for Christ will last – that was my father's life as he lived it out.

Charles Clifton Querry's earthly presence will be seen throughout the remainder of eternity in the people and places he touched. Each of you: family members, friends, fellow ministers, and those whose lives have been impacted by my father, can attest to that fact.

A few days after Pop received a personally escorted journey to his reward, I was musing about what Pop's Heavenly Welcoming Committee must have looked like at 5:05 am on Thursday, June 22nd.

I can only imagine what the streets of gold looked like as it was lined with throngs of cheering saints. Those assembled included his parents, his brothers and sisters, fellow ministers, those men and women he pastored throughout the years, and those who Pop personally led to the Lord.

But I can also imagine that Jesus reminded them all that He is the Alpha and the Omega and that He would be the first and the last one to welcome and embrace my Father.

Charles Querry, in your seventy-nine years, you left your fingerprints all over your earthly home and on those you loved.

1. **In The Places He Pastored!**
    Pop's fingerprints can be seen in the twenty-one churches he shepherded in six different states in fifty-four years of pastoral ministry.
    † Madras, Reedsport, and Salem, Oregon;
    † Coeur d' Alene, and Lewiston, Idaho;
    † Bakersfield, Baldwin Park, Hercules, Long Beach, Oroville, Porterville, Riverside, San Martin, San Pablo, Visalia (twice), Salinas, and Watsonville, California;
    † Las Vegas, Nevada;
    † Grand Junction, Colorado; and
    † Aurora and Logan, Illinois.
    Many of these churches were in trouble, in a decline, or had to be resurrected when Charles Querry led his family to minister in and to these cities. And they were healthy and thriving when he answered the call for the next assignment.

    Every place he and mom called home and a place to serve has a little bit of his blood, sweat, tears, and a whole lot of his heart. I'm pretty sure that at every church they pastored, my father's fingerprints can be seen in the buildings he built, and in the classrooms, sanctuaries, fellowship halls, and parsonages he personally remodeled.

I think he loved being a carpenter for the Great Carpenter.

2. **In The People He Shepherded!**
Fifty-two years of pastoral ministry – wow!

How many thousands of individuals did Pop touch with his strong hands and gentle heart.

My parents officially retired three times, yet in each case, once my father received the call that another church needed a loving shepherd, off they went again. He could never reject the call to go and minister to another congregation of hurting sheep. I joked with Pop on a number of occasions that his and mom's ministry had been so successful but that they really sucked at retirement. (smiles)

There was a passion and love for people that burned deep within the heart of Charles Querry. He really cared for and deeply loved each of you. You became part of our family.

He called your name out in prayer in the early mornings sitting in his chair after his personal time with his Savior.

He sat with you in hospitals, ate meals with you, laughed with you, cried with you, he sacrificed his life for you, he led and shepherded you.

For some, he introduced you to Jesus; for some, he helped you experience a deeper relationship with Christ; for some, he assisted you in opening the Gift of the Holy Spirit in your daily journey; for others, he encouraged and supported you to minister within your calling and gifting.

Of all the fingerprints Pop left on this world, I think leading someone to Christ was his favorite. Seeing someone experience salvation gave validation to the sacrifice he gave to "Go into All the World." He did all of that because he really loved you. He was a father to many of you.

One particularly moving tribute we received recently ended with this statement, "Thank you for sharing your Pop with the world." It has truly been overwhelming to read and hear the number of people who call my Pop, "Pop" or say he was their spiritual father or grandfather.

3. **In The Pastors He Mentored!**
As our family was discussing Pop and his legacy, his mentoring and training of pastors, the decision was made to establish a scholarship fund to train men and women who sense the call of God upon their lives.

There are hundreds of men and women in ministry today in whom Charles Querry poured his knowledge and life. He was a spiritual father who believed in lovingly sharing his ministry experience. He was a trainer, a supervisor, a leader, and a mentor in many Ministerial Internship Programs.

There are dozens of churches thriving today that are pastored by children and teenagers he pastored and poured his life into. He wasn't afraid to take a chance on a young man or woman that many had already given up on, he just lovingly spent time with them, discipled and loved them.

One of the greatest testaments of his desire to create leaders is seen in his family. My father believed everyone is called into a ministry, and some of those ministries would actually occur inside of a church.

My father knew that his first leadership mentoring calling was to his family. He convinced us that our ministry was to lead and to create leaders amongst those we lead.

His wife, Linda (my mother), is a leader of leaders as the newly appointed Senior Pastor of the Grove Avenue Church of God in Visalia, California.

Rodney is a leader of leaders as an Executive Pastor at the Calvary Church of the Quad Cities in Moline, Illinois.

Randy is a leader of leaders as a Police Lieutenant at the Newport Beach Police Department in Newport Beach, California.

Kevin is a leader of leaders as Co-Lead Pastor at Living Waters Christian Fellowship in Fountain Valley, California.

His daughters-in-love and each of his grandchildren are leaders of leaders in ministry and in the workforce, and I'm convinced his great-grandchildren will be leaders of leaders because that's the legacy Pop left us.

One of the most moving and personally rewarding conversations I have ever had with my daughter, Aubrey, took place last Friday. I was in Quito, Ecuador training Ecuadorian Pastors, and Aubrey and I had a FaceTime conversation. Aubrey expressed to me that she had made the decision to enter into the California/Nevada Ministerial Internship Program this fall. She wanted, as Charles Querry's granddaughter, to be the first recipient of the Charles Querry Ministerial Internship Scholarship to honor her Poppa.

A legacy of leaders leading leaders.

Pop's Fingerprints!

4. **In The Family He Loved and Led!**
    The person Charles Querry was in the pulpit or around a State Council Board table was the same person he was playing golf, watching his boys play softball, or at home being Pop and Poppa.

Charles Querry was authentic. One of his greatest characteristics was that he always led humbly.

As a matter of fact, we are still finding out things (even this week) that he accomplished while in the Navy that he was too humble to share, even with mom. If he was physically present today, he would tell us to knock off all this stuff, stop fussing all over me, 'cause that just wasn't his style.

You all know that my father was just fun to be around; he was a jokester. As children, growing up around my father was fun. Every scratch or scar he had on his body; we were told happened because he was shot in the war.

He loved to laugh and encouraged all of us to laugh at ourselves and not take ourselves too seriously. He made life an adventure.

We never knew that spending the night in the car at a roadside rest stop was due to our being poor ... it was an adventure.

Getting stranded on Christmas Day between Western Illinois and Eastern Missouri heading to Oregon was an adventure.

Now, I realize that the windows freezing on the inside of the car and Stretch Armstrong freezing solid were signs that we were in trouble.

The backseat of a patrol car with its heater on was the best place in the world that night – maybe that's why Randy is a cop today.

He made life fun and adventurous because he loved his family. I mean he really loved each one of us. He loved us the same, but he loved us differently.

He knew how to interact with his 50+ year-old sons, his 27-year-old grandsons, his 10-year-old granddaughter, his two-year-old great-grandson, his 12-week-old great-granddaughter, and every one of us in between. And he had a special place in that huge heart of his where every one of us fit! He took time with each of us to have special inside jokes, tickle our ribs, or sing silly songs ... to name just a couple:

- ♥ Oh, They Call It That Good Ole Mountain Dew – (verses and all), and
- ♥ I Was Looking Back to See If You Were Looking Back to See If I Was Looking Back to See If You Were Looking Back at Me.

He took the time to invest in us all, to allow his finger-prints to imprint on our hearts and lives.

We walk with a bounce, we carry his hairline, and many more characteristics that are too many to share.

Pop taught us so many things.

He taught us to love Jesus and people.

He taught us to love regardless of color or economic position.

He taught us to respect mom and our elders.

He taught us to honor him as our father.

He taught us to be authentic.

He taught us a good work ethic ... something about a man shouldn't eat if he doesn't work ... don't know where he got that idea.

He taught us to play cards, specifically Rook, Trip-oli, and Poker – for fun, of course – no gambling for us. Will you indulge me and allow me to tell you a quick Querry family story?

The day Pop graduated into Heaven, we did what the Querry's do when difficult seasons hit us, we gathered together. We ate dinner, watched some old family movies, we laughed, we cried, and then one of the grandkids said, "...let's play poker in honor of Pop." We pulled out the table, the chips, and the cards ... Yes, we have them all.

Remember, we were taught to be authentic!

We even convinced mom to play with us.

I won't go into the gory details, but let me just say mom had a little assistance from someone with a better vantage point that night. She proceeded to out-hand every one of us around the table until she possessed all the chips. If you had two pairs, she had trips; if you had trips, she had a larger set of trips.

Pop always loved her more.

Pop's greatest fingerprints can be seen in the lives of his family.

What does it profit a man if he gains the whole world and loses his own family?

That was not to be Charles Querry's legacy!

Pop understood his first priority was to his family. He may not have made all the games, concerts, or all of the right decisions. He may have had to sacrifice family time and vacations because of ministry responsibilities, but he did his very best. He may not have been perfect, although he was pretty close in our eyes, but he did a lot of things right.

The fingerprints that mean the most to Charles Querry right now is that every member of his family lineage has a personal relationship with Jesus Christ. He shared Jesus with each of us through his life. He lived Christ out loud and taught us through his example that loving and living for Jesus was critical. He understood that he couldn't stop working on his relationship with Christ because there were a number of us watching him. He knew that just because we were raised in a pastor's home didn't mean that our eternal home would be Heaven, so he had to walk the walk as well as talk the talk.

He prayed for each of us to fulfill the destiny and the leadership calling that God had determined for us. Pop was always on our sidelines being our cheerleader, and now he's cheering us on from the best seats in the house. I can hear him saying to each of us: Keep your chin up! Don't give up! Don't quit! The battle is almost over!

Let's continue to make him proud, Querry's, by loving each other, serving God, and leading in the callings, capacity, and communities we now live.

Today, I speak for my brothers. We feel like we did as little kids stepping into your shoes after Sunday services and attempting to stroll around the room. You have left huge shoes to fill, and we commit to working every day to be the husband, father, grandfather, great-grandfather, pastor, mentor, leader, and friend that you were. We feel like preschoolers finger painting, attempting to recreate the masterpiece your fingers created everywhere you served.

We commit in reverence to God and in honor of you to live our lives loving Jesus and loving people like you loved them; to continue walking and strengthening our faith; and to take care of one another because when life gets hard ... family is a soft place to land.

Pop, you are and will forever be missed. We love you, and we will see you again very soon.

Querry's ... We are Pop's Fingerprints!

• • • • • • • • • • • • • • • • •

Written by Randy, our second son, June 22, 2017

Well, this great man of God went home to get his reward at 5:05 this morning. His family and friends knew him as Pop, Poppa, and Uncle Chuck. Many other close friends knew him as Pastor Q, Pastor Querry, Pastor Chuck, Reverend Querry, and on and on. I can't tell you how blessed I have been to have him as my father. He has been the ultimate role model. I wanted to share some facts about this great man that many never knew.

My Pop dropped out of high school in the 11th grade at age 17 and lied on his application to go into the Navy. He served his country for four years at the end of the Korean War. He was quite the jokester! Pop had many scars, and as kids, when we would ask him about those scars, his reply was always, "I got shot in the war." If those were true, he would have had about 50 Purple Hearts! Ha.

Growing up and prior to meeting my mom, he was quite the hellion. The Querry family were quite the hellions growing up. Pop always said they would fight at the drop of a hat, and normally one of them would drop the hat, ha! His life during his Navy days involved drinking and fighting. As he said, it was something he looked forward to. He fought so much that they asked him to join their boxing team. He joined and proceeded, as he said, to get his tail kicked. He stopped and said he doesn't have "rules" the way he fights, ha! When he met and started dating my mother, that all stopped. He literally quit smoking and drinking on the spot. He gave his heart to God and shortly thereafter became a licensed minister. He spent the next fifty-four years preaching God's word. This is the Pop most everyone knows. This man would never speak a bad word about anyone, would give you the shirt off of his back, and simply loved to love people. From the most dignified to the homeless, he hugged, prayed with/for, and loved anyone that crossed his path.

A high school dropout is something that didn't define Pop. He went back to school, got his GED, and continued until he obtained his Doctorate degree. Yes, Dr. Charles Querry. To me, he was the most talented and determined man I knew. He was a carpenter in the Navy and continued using those talents over the years. Pop built several houses from the ground up, some by himself. Those of you who had the pleasure of having him as your Pastor know that he remodeled just about every church and/or parsonage they went to. He and many others built the church in Bakersfield known as Southwest Christian Center.

Pop was very athletic and quite the basketball and baseball player. Personally, I truly think Pop could have been a professional athlete in either sport. Those who played with or competed against him during his younger days can contest to that. He played basketball with and against some who went on to play in the pros. When my brothers and I played against Pop, he never held back. He wanted you to learn the game and push yourself to get better. I was 21 years old when I finally beat Pop in a basketball game of 21. If you do the math, Pop was 50! That either shows how pathetic I was or how good he was, HA! As a kid going to church youth camps, my Pop became the most sought-after minister to come pick up the kids. On the last day of youth camp (Friday), the kids would always play the counselors in a game of softball. One year Pop arrived to pick up the youth, and we were playing a game. The kids started chanting for Pastor Querry to bat. During those days, we only had wooden bats. Pop came to the plate with slacks and dress shoes on and, as a joke, flipped the bat around and held the barrel of the bat in his hands. They pitched the ball, and Pop hit the ball with the handle of the bat and literally knocked the ball out of the park. We were all stunned. Every year after, it became a tradition. Pop would show up on Friday, the kids and now counselors would call to him, they'd pitch the ball, and I kid you not, every single time he knocked the ball out of the park. You can't imagine how proud my brothers and I were. That was our dad!!! Pop was 72 (7 years ago) when he came to watch one of our softball games. We were having batting practice, and I asked Pop if he wanted to bat. He came up to bat, I pitched to him, and he literally hit line drive after line drive into the field. Several on the team jokingly asked for batting lessons. When you've got it, you've got it!

Right now, there is a celebration going on in Heaven. Pop is hugging and loving on his family and friends he has lost over the years. He will always be remembered as a loving, caring man! I will always love you Pop, and know you will always be with us!!!

• • • • • • • • • • • • • • • • • •

Written by Rodney, our third son, June 22, 2017

My father, Charles Querry, heard words this morning at 5:05 AM that he's preached about for fifty-plus years, "...well done, thou good and faithful Servant...enter into the joy of the Lord."

My brothers and I SHARED my dad with people all across the United States. It was always a joy to hear one of my friends call him "Pop." Dad was always welcoming to everyone with a big hug and lots of love to go around.

Kevin and Randy posted phenomenal tributes to Dad, be sure to read them. But Dad's legacy lives on through his wife, his sons, his daughters-in-law, his grandchildren, and many of you who were touched by his life and ministry.

We've been in ministry our whole lives, and today, WE are experiencing grief and sadness while rejoicing that Pop is no longer in pain. We have held your hands while crying and praying with you through the years and now are asking for your comfort and love back to us.

So, with tears in my eyes, I hum Dad's favorite hymn,
**" Then sings my soul, my Savior God to Thee.
How great Thou art. How great Thou art.
Then sings my soul, my Savior God to Thee.
How great Thou art. How great Thou art. "** [16]

---

16 How Great Thou Art, is a Christian hymn based on an original Swedish hymn entitled "O Store Gud" written in 1885 by Carl Boberg; the English version of the hymn and its title are a loose translation by the English missionary Stuart K. Hine from 1949

I love the image in my mind of Dad singing that as he entered Heaven.

I will miss our morning chats, our morning breakfasts finding the best biscuits and gravy in town, and your positive outlook that sometimes irritated me. I always just wanted you to get mad one time. (smiles) You've left a legacy.

❝ There will be a happy meeting in heaven I know.
When we see the many loved ones, we've known here below.
Gathered on that blessed hilltop with hearts all aglow.
That will be a glad reunion day.
Glad day, a wonderful day.
Glad day, a glorious day.
There will all the holy angels and loved ones to stay.
That will be a glad reunion day. **❞** [17]

I'd like to close this chapter with a song dedicated to my three sons, Kevin, Randy and Rodney.

"Even though I'm leaving"
Daddy, I'm afraid, won't you stay a little while?
Keep me safe 'cause there's monsters right outside.
Daddy, please don't go, I don't wanna be alone
'Cause the second that you're gone they're gonna know
Before he went to bed, he grabbed my hand and said
Just 'cause I'm leavin'
It don't mean that I won't be right by your side
When you need me,
and you can't see me in the middle of the night
Just close your eyes and say a prayer
It's okay, I know you're scared when I'm not there
Even though I'm leavin', I ain't goin' nowhere.

---

17 Songwriter: Adger M. Pace

Dad, we'll be late, and Uncle Sam don't like to wait
He's got a big old plane that's gonna take me far away
I know I act tough, but there's a churnin' in my gut
'Cause I just can't call you up when things get rough
Before I left, he hugged my neck and said,
Just "cause you're leavin'
It don't mean that I won't be right by your side
When you need me in the middle of the night
Just close your eyes and say a prayer
It's okay, I know you're scared,
I might be here, But I'll always be right there
Even though you're leavin', I ain't going nowhere.

Daddy, I'm afraid, won't you stay a little while?
I never thought I'd see the day I had to say goodbye
Daddy, please don't go, I can't do this on my own
There's no way that I can walk this road alone
Well, daddy grabbed my hand and said,
Just 'cause I'm leavin'
It don't mean that I won't be right by your side
When you need me
And you can't see me in the middle of the night
Just close your eyes and say a prayer
It's okay, boy, I ain't scared
I won't be here, but I'll always be right there
Even though I'm leavin', I ain't goin' nowhere!
I ain't goin' nowhere![18]

---

18 Songwriters: Luke Combs / Ray Fulcher / Wyatt Durrette
Blackstone entertainment, Song/ATV Music Publishing LLC, Warner Chappell Music, Inc

Chapter 22

life's a dance you learn as you go!

John Michael Montgomery sings a song entitled,
"Life's a Dance,"
> *Life's a dance, you learn as you go,*
> *sometimes you lead, sometimes you follow.*
> *Don't worry about what you don't know,*
> *Life's a dance you learn as you go.*[19]

I wish I could end this book and say, "It is OVER! It doesn't hurt ANYMORE!" But those words will never be a part of my story. I cannot even say that after five years, it is easier.

I find myself staying up late at night with the TV on because I know when I wake up in the morning, he will still be gone, and I am still alone to face my day. I still sleep with his picture beside me. Sometimes I just hold it all night. Even though I know he is not coming back, it makes me feel close to him when I sleep.

I now know survival isn't easy, but it is possible. As I look back, I find myself relating these years to my life in high

---

19   Songwriters: Steve Jay Seskin / James Allen Shamblin

school. In the beginning stage, I really was not sure I would make it – or even wanted to. It was like the first semester of my "freshman" year. I was wandering around in this big ole world, trying to find the place where I was going to fit in. I was now meeting new friends, and these new friends never knew the "old me" that I had been all those years before.

Year two, my sophomore year, I am a little more acquainted with this new "school/life" that I entered last year. I am missing those "junior-high school" friends I had known for a long time. Some of them have moved on – away from the weepy me. They still have their companions, and they are just not sure how to help me through this season of my life. But I have made some new friends, and I have shared my story with some. Some of them have lost their soulmate, too, so they can relate a little to my loss. But remember this, everybody's loss is on their own "Richter scale." The earthquake magnitudes are variable. Some have aftershocks for a very long time, and some settle down much faster. That doesn't mean their loss is any less than yours. That only means "our" loss is just that – "ours!" Don't regulate yours on someone else's scale.

Year three was my "junior" year. I had become acquainted quite well with this journey now. I knew there were people and places that sent me in a downward spiral, and I tried to avoid that. I have spent many hours trying to learn how to motivate just "me" now. Oh, the hard tests still come. The hours of just stealing away to be by myself and try to find my place again still happens I find myself fearful as each year is coming to an end and what I might have to face in the next year. Everything seems so final now. My whole foundation crumbled around me in my freshman year, but

I have amazed myself that I have gotten this far. The pain has not lessened, and I am pretty sure it never will. In fact, it may have even intensified. But I cry, most of the time, a little softer and, at times, even farther between. I find myself having those gut-wrenching cries now hidden away in my room at night with my face buried in my pillow to stifle the sound, or if the pressure builds to where I see it coming, I will get in the car and park in some secluded area of a parking lot and scream out the pain. That HeartPAIN has not left, but it is definitely different. The wound from my heart being split in two, still aches and I wonder, at times, will it ever heal?

Year four, my "senior" year. I have realized over and over again the "me" that entered as a freshman – scared, fearful, insecure, unsure - is gone now. There is this new me trying desperately to find where I am going from here. What do I do? At the end of this year, where will I be? I am more tender now. I am crushed easier. I fight to become that secure, sure person I was when he was by my side. I cry so easily. I see things differently now than I have ever seen them before. I cherish my moments with family more than ever. I find myself fighting depression more now than ever in the previous three years. This year I moved eighteen hundred miles away to live with my youngest son and his family. I gave up my home. Even though my son and daughter-in-law have been great, my life has changed. My finances changed. My work changed. My health changed. I have had to face and accept the reality that "changes" have become part of the "new me" that exists in this life now. It is not easy. It is just what it is. So, I have to answer the question, where do I go at the end of this year?

Year five, maybe this is what endless college years feel like – it is about learning, and learning some more, and then some more. One thing I have been so grateful for is that I have had God to walk this journey with me. In my worst fears, in my most insecure times, in the toughest moments, fighting changes, fighting depression, fighting a dam-over-flow of tears, it has been God, right there in those moments, that has brought me through them. I have had to trust Him in my life – every moment of my life. I don't think I ever realized how dependent I was on my husband until he was gone. Chuck used to tell me, "You are the most independent dependent woman I've ever known." Guilty! SO GUILTY! And I am not so sure, if I could "humanly" see God react like us humans, I'm sure at times, with His hands over His face, shaking his head, He's said the same thing about me.

I want so bad to be able to read that book God wrote about me before I was born. I want so bad to see His plan for me. I want so bad to know what my tomorrows hold. I want so bad at times just to go to heaven and be reunited with my love. But I do not know any of these. As bad as I want to know what my future holds, I don't. But I will never stop being determined to live my life to the fullest and serving God with everything that is in me. Yes, even in times when I feel like He is a million miles away from me, even at times of darkness when I feel like my prayers cannot break through, even when my prayers are not answered "yet," I will cling to God's hands, as he holds me as I walk this journey of grief no one asks to take.

This book, "grief, how long will you linger?" ... does not have the answer. Maybe it's like that glitter; it will always be somewhere lingering in a corner, appearing at times when you thought it was all gone. Maybe it's like a scar. Scars are a sign of what tried to kill you but didn't. These scars are a testament that I loved deeply. I experienced cuts or even gouges, but I survived those and continued to live and love. Those scars may be ugly to people, but they're a reminder to me that even through the tough times, we loved each other deeply.

Losing my husband shook my world! It changed who I was. It's been like a wild ride these past few years, going so fast it has blown my hair out of place. Yet, here I am today, still standing upright. In all those fifty-two years as pastors, and the four years I served as a pastor after Chuck left for heaven, through times of deaths and funerals for family and for those we knew and pastored, through leadership classes, throughout both of our careers, nothing and no one prepared me for what I have faced in these five years of grief.

Nothing prepared me to be knocked off my feet grieving the loss of my soulmate. No one taught a class on this. No one! Why haven't there been classes for pastors, for ministers, so they could better help their parishioners going through these times? Why hasn't someone done something to help me, as a Pastor's wife and now a retired pastor, to know what to expect and how to face this horrific journey? The people who meet me now and become a part of my life will not have had the pleasure of knowing that happy, secure person I was in crowds, or speaking at conventions, or at dinner parties when he was beside me. If he was here, I could go through this journey with flying colors. If he was here, I would not be afraid. If he was here, I would be proud to walk into strange and unknown places because he would hold my hand all the way. But he is not here. So, that me, that person, died too. I am crippled by this amputation of part of me that is gone. I've survived, so far, being dropped into this jungle of grief in one brief moment.

When you see me, I am walking differently now. I am not that same person I was five and a half years ago. But take note, I am not giving up. I will now dance with a limp. But I will dance anyway because "life's a dance, you learn as you go."

Chapter 23

from the end...to the beginning

R ecently while traveling in my car to an appointment, this song came on the radio. It had been quite a while since I have had to pull off the road because my tears were blinding me. But by end of the first verse, there I was, in a parking lot, bawling my eyes out...wishing for one more day with the love of my life.

One More Day
Last night I had a crazy dream
A wish was granted just for me. It could be for anything
I didn't ask for money, Or a mansion in Malibu
I simply wised for one more day with you.

First thing I'd do is pray for time to crawl
I'd unplug the telephone and keep the TV off
I'd hold you every second, say a million I love you's
That's what I'd do with one more day with you.

One more day, one more time
One more sunset, maybe I'd be satisfied

> But then again, I know what it would do
> Leave me wishing still for one more day with you
> One more day with you.[20]

I vividly remember on my wedding day my mom making this comment. "Linda, little did I know that on that cold October day when you were born, there was a little eight-year-old boy running through the cotton patches in Arkansas that would grow up to be the man you would marry. All I have ever wanted for you was for you to be happy." That day was the beginning of fifty-four years, two months, and ten days of happy times. I was marrying the man who would go to great lengths to see that I was happy.

When my husband's heart stopped beating early that Thursday morning, my "happy" left this world with him. My whole being, my entire family, was shaken to the core. Our hero's life had ended here on this earth, but he was starting his new beginning, with his next heartbeat in his eternal home in heaven. I watched as my sons and their families returned to their jobs, as we all struggled to figure out what, where, and how do we keep going? We were in shock, moving in slow motion. Yet this world never missed a beat; not a second on the clock stopped or changed. Those seconds turned into minutes, then hours, then days, months, and now years. But the one thing that kept us moving forward was knowing we would do what Chuck, what their Pop, would tell us to do, "Keep Your Chin Up!" Grief struck us like that sledgehammer I mentioned earlier. It invaded our thoughts, our actions, and our lives. When a day before, we were ready to conquer, twenty-four hours later, our world had flipped

---

20 Sung by Diamond Rio; Songwriters: Bobby Wayne Tomberlin/Steven D. Jones

upside down. We were shattered. Our hopes had just come crumbling down.

As I've written this book, the lower-case lettering of the titles just felt like that was the way it should be. As I reflect back on it now, perhaps it was my subconscious mind, maybe it was God, or possibly it was a personal message for me stating, "grief, you will not overpower me!" As I began to research some of the reasons people write with all lower-case letters, it all began to make sense. One reason was it communicates "endlessness." It signals familiarity as if to say, "We know each other; we are comfortable being here because we understand." There that's it. This grief is endless, but I refuse to let it have power over me, to control me. In every chapter, I was comfortable being there because I was writing about this journey of grief that I understood. When I speak to someone now who has lost the love of their life, even though their grief is "theirs," there is a part of me that understands those tears they're shedding.

As I close this final chapter, let me say this, without a doubt I know there will be more days of tears. Some days are just harder than others, regardless of where you're at in your loss. I fight depression, but I determined after the first few months, I will refuse to let depression conquer me. Depression brings on guilt and feelings of inadequacy. We wrestle with the "what if I had only. . ." We can "what if" 'til the cows come home' (that just might be a southern slang-smiles), and it doesn't change a thing...I know; I did it. Grief will attempt to oppress you. Oppress literally means 'to wear away' or 'wear out,' as one would wear out a garment. Grieve as you feel you must but don't allow "grief" to destroy you, to wear you out where you are no good for anyone or anything.

You may not feel it at first, I certainly did not, but if you're still breathing, there's more for you to do here. God's book about you isn't finished. God doesn't place us here just to suck up air. He has a place He designed with "YOU" in mind.

What looked like "the end" when I lost my sweetheart was not only his "new beginning," but it was also mine. I am not sure yet what that place looks like for me. But until I find that "happy" me again, I refuse to allow grief to over-power me.

Stephen Hoeller wrote this: A pearl is a beautiful thing that is produced by an injured life. It is the tear [that results] from the injury of the oyster. The treasure of our being in this world is also produced by an injured life. If we had not been wounded, if we had not been injured, then we would not produce the pearl."

There will be more times – like the song - of wishing I had one more day with you Babe, and that most likely will not go away. But until I have that one more day and days and days for eternity with you in heaven, this broken heart, my injured life, that has punctured my inner being, I choose to be like that oyster, and with God by my side, I will produce a pearl.

Psalm 28:7 [NRSV] – The Lord is my strength and my shield; in him my heart trusts, and I am helped...

Jeremiah 29:11 [NIV] – "For I know the plans I have for you,' declares the Lord, 'plans to prosper you and not harm you, plans to give you hope and a future."

And one of my "go-to" scriptures so many times these past five and a half years is where God promises to meet you in your pain and to help you, saying, *"So do not fear, for I am with you; do not be dismayed, for I am your God. I will strengthen you and help you; I will uphold you with my righteous right hand."* Isaiah 41:10 [NIV]

Those are promises that we aren't walking this journey by ourselves. God is right there with us. Cling to them as you go and make your pearl until you join your loved one, not for just one more day, but for eternity.

Scholarship Fund

Shortly after my husband passed away, as my family gathered together to make decisions that we knew would make him happy, we all decided to set up a Ministerial Intern Program (MIP) Scholarship Fund in his name. A program he not only believed in and taught in for 12 years, but encouraged many young men and women to become a part of. If you would like to make a donation to this, you can do so by mailing a check to the following address or going online and donating. Please always specify your donation to: "Charles Querry MIP Scholarship Fund." All donations are tax deductible.

Donations may be mailed to:
Church of God State Executive Offices
PO BOX 26058
Fresno, CA 93729-6058

Or to the street address:
6901 Maple Avenue
Fresno, CA 93729

Or online at:
canvcog.com
(go to online giving / offering and gifts / Charles Querry Scholarship)

About the Author

Linda Querry is an Ordained Minister of the Church of God. She ministers to others out of the passion and devotion she has for Christ and believes there is no struggle that threatens your "God-given" assignment that you can't overcome with God on your side. You'll find her refreshing and entertaining as she ministers through illustrated sermons sharing the anointed Word of God.

Linda has served as a Conference & Retreat speaker, Teacher, Music Director, Workshop instructor, Singer, and Pianist throughout the United States during 56 years of ministry. Both Linda and her husband, Dr. Charles Querry, served as Lead Pastors for 52 years in the Church of God. After his homegoing on June 22, 2017, Linda continued to serve as Lead Pastor for the next 4 years at the church where they were pastoring. She retired in June 2021 from Visalia, California, and relocated to McKinney, Texas, where she serves in various groups at Elevate Life Church with Pastor Keith Craft.

Linda is available for speaking engagements as a Conference or Retreat speaker or to minister in your church at any time. You may contact her at lcquerry@yahoo.com.

If you would like to order copies of her book, *"grief, how long will you linger here?"* scan the QR code:

http://www.thearcuegroup.com/